Image Retrieval and Analysis Using Text and Fuzzy Shape Features:

Emerging Research and Opportunities

P. Sumathy
Bharathidasan University, India

P. Shanmugavadivu
Gandhigram Rural Institute, India

A. Vadivel
National Institute of Technology Tiruchirappalli, India

A volume in the Advances in
Multimedia and Interactive
Technologies (AMIT) Book Series

Published in the United States of America by
        IGI Global
        Information Science Reference (an imprint of IGI Global)
        701 E. Chocolate Avenue
        Hershey PA, USA 17033
        Tel: 717-533-8845
        Fax: 717-533-8661
        E-mail: cust@igi-global.com
        Web site: http://www.igi-global.com

Library of Congress Cataloging-in-Publication Data

Names: Sumathy, P., 1975- author. | Shanmugavadivu, P., 1967- author. |
   Vadivel, A., 1979- author.
Title: Image retrieval and analysis using text and fuzzy shape features :
   emerging research and opportunities / by P. Sumathy, P. Shanmugavadivu,
   and A. Vadivel.
Description: Hershey, PA : Information Science Reference, [2018] | Includes
   bibliographical references.
Identifiers: LCCN 2017022537| ISBN 9781522537960 (hardcover) | ISBN
   9781522537977 (ebook)
Subjects: LCSH: Image analysis. | Fuzzy systems. | Content-based image
   retrieval.
Classification: LCC TA1637 .S786 2018 | DDC 006.4/2--dc23 LC record available at https://lccn.
loc.gov/2017022537

This book is published in the IGI Global book series Advances in Multimedia and Interactive Technologies (AMIT) (ISSN: 2327-929X; eISSN: 2327-9303)

British Cataloguing in Publication Data
A Cataloguing in Publication record for this book is available from the British Library.

All work contributed to this book is new, previously-unpublished material.
The views expressed in this book are those of the authors, but not necessarily of the publisher.

For electronic access to this publication, please contact: eresources@igi-global.com.

Advances in Multimedia and Interactive Technologies (AMIT) Book Series

ISSN:2327-929X
EISSN:2327-9303

Editor-in-Chief: Joel J.P.C. Rodrigues, National Institute of Telecommunications (Inatel), Brazil & Instituto de Telecomunicações, University of Beira Interior, Portugal

MISSION

Traditional forms of media communications are continuously being challenged. The emergence of user-friendly web-based applications such as social media and Web 2.0 has expanded into everyday society, providing an interactive structure to media content such as images, audio, video, and text.

The **Advances in Multimedia and Interactive Technologies (AMIT) Book Series** investigates the relationship between multimedia technology and the usability of web applications. This series aims to highlight evolving research on interactive communication systems, tools, applications, and techniques to provide researchers, practitioners, and students of information technology, communication science, media studies, and many more with a comprehensive examination of these multimedia technology trends.

COVERAGE
- Digital Games
- Audio Signals
- Multimedia Technology
- Web Technologies
- Internet Technologies
- Digital Images
- Social Networking
- Multimedia Services
- Digital Watermarking
- Multimedia Streaming

IGI Global is currently accepting manuscripts for publication within this series. To submit a proposal for a volume in this series, please contact our Acquisition Editors at Acquisitions@igi-global.com or visit: http://www.igi-global.com/publish/.

Titles in this Series

For a list of additional titles in this series, please visit:
https://www.igi-global.com/book-series/advances-multimedia-interactive-technologies/73683

Handbook of Research on Advanced Concepts in Real-Time Image and Video Processing
Md. Imtiyaz Anwar (National Institute of Technology, Jalandhar, India) Arun Khosla (National Institute of Technology, Jalandhar, India) and Rajiv Kapoor (Delhi Technological University, India)
Information Science Reference • ©2018 • 504pp • H/C (ISBN: 9781522528487) • US $265.00

Transforming Gaming and Computer Simulation Technologies across Industries
Brock Dubbels (McMaster University, Canada)
Information Science Reference • ©2017 • 297pp • H/C (ISBN: 9781522518174) • US $210.00

Feature Detectors and Motion Detection in Video Processing
Nilanjan Dey (Techno India College of Technology, Kolkata, India) Amira Ashour (Tanta University, Egypt) and Prasenjit Kr. Patra (Bengal College of Engineering and Technology, India)
Information Science Reference • ©2017 • 328pp • H/C (ISBN: 9781522510253) • US $200.00

Mobile Application Development, Usability, and Security
Sougata Mukherjea (IBM, India)
Information Science Reference • ©2017 • 320pp • H/C (ISBN: 9781522509455) • US $180.00

Applied Video Processing in Surveillance and Monitoring Systems
Nilanjan Dey (Techno India College of Technology, Kolkata, India) Amira Ashour (Tanta University, Egypt) and Suvojit Acharjee (National Institute of Technology Agartala, India)
Information Science Reference • ©2017 • 321pp • H/C (ISBN: 9781522510222) • US $215.00

Intelligent Analysis of Multimedia Information
Siddhartha Bhattacharyya (RCC Institute of Information Technology, India) Hrishikesh Bhaumik (RCC Institute of Information Technology, India) Sourav De (The University of Burdwan, India) and Goran Klepac (University College for Applied Computer Engineering Algebra, Croatia & Raiffeisenbank Austria, Croatia)
Information Science Reference • ©2017 • 520pp • H/C (ISBN: 9781522504986) • US $220.00

For an enitre list of titles in this series, please visit:
https://www.igi-global.com/book-series/advances-multimedia-interactive-technologies/73683

701 East Chocolate Avenue, Hershey, PA 17033, USA
Tel: 717-533-8845 x100 • Fax: 717-533-8661
E-Mail: cust@igi-global.com • www.igi-global.com

Table of Contents

Preface

INTRODUCTION

The ever-growing potential of internet is exponentially increasing the scope and applications of Multimedia Information Retrieval Systems which in turn has triggered the development of novel and robust techniques for extracting contextually relevant text and/or images. The issues and challenges associated with the information retrieval systems for World Wide Web (WWW) has led to the emergence of a new dimension in the domain of Text Based Image Retrieval (TBIR) and Content Based Image Retrieval (CBIR) Systems. The effectiveness of any information retrieval systems is governed by two primary features namely, contextual precision of the information to be extracted and the time duration of retrieval. As the population of images used by various applications is growing explosively, there is compelling demand on the researchers to evolve newer techniques for image retrieval, which would outperform the existing ones. This book presents new ideas and techniques on image retrieval.

ABOUT THE BOOK

This book brings together an identifiable 'core' of Image Retrieval (IR) ideas, techniques, and applications using text based and content based approaches. It is indented for researchers working in the field of Content-Based Image Retrieval and Text-Based Image Retrieval are the target audience. It is the outgrowth of graduate course taught in the Department of Computer Engineering and Information Technology. We realized the need to the research scholars who are working in the field of Image Retrieval using the content of image and textual information and as a result it is a combined product made up of Text Based Image Retrieval and Content Based Image Retrieval.

The novel text based and content-based concept of image handling needs to be integrated with more traditional semantics. Image Retrieval focuses on the tools of processing and searching applicable to the content-based management of new multimedia documents.

ORGANIZATION OF THE BOOK

This book contains six chapters and the details of the book are presented as follows.

Chapter 1 discusses introduction to TBIR and CBIR with suitable example and application domains. It also presents related theories and puts forward new methodologies along with the results and analysis. It explains newly developed method for ranking the images in Web documents based on the properties of HTML TAGS in web documents for image retrieval from WWW.

Chapter 2 presents CBIR methodologies for extracting geometric and margin features of objects in images. Various properties of objects are calculated and constructed as feature vector. This approach is unique in nature as the size of the feature is relatively small and capable of discriminating the query object with the datbase object. The performance of the feature is tested in CBIR application using precision and recall metrics.

This method is extended in Chapter 3 by estimating the fuzziness associated with the geometric and margin properties of objects in images. The Fuzzy-Object-Shape (FOS) feature of images are extracted for each object. The closeness of each object with primitive shapes is estimated using fuzzy membership function and constructed as feature vector. The FOS technique is divised out of this research study that explores fuzzy shapes to capture the shape of an object of interest along with the degree of impreciseness in the boundary information which provides a measure of closeness of the object of interest with reference to the well-known shapes and the similarity measure.

Indexing is very important for image retrieval applications. It is imperative that a suitable indexing mechanism is required for effectively indexing low-level feature. The indexed feature can be combined with textual feature for facilitating shape based retrieval in Chapter 4. In addition, a Fuzzy-Object-Level image matching algorithm is proposed for measuring the similarity between the query and database images.

The working principle of proposed similarity measure is explained in Chapter 5 for measuring the degree of closeness of objects present in both query and database images. A Common Bin Similarity Measure (CBSM) is proposed for ranking the images using the encoded feature.

A suitable indexing mechanism that combines the text features with shape features (encoded and normal) for text-shape based retrieval is proposed in Chapter 6. This technique combines the text information with the shape information to enhance the retrieval performance. In addition, this method encode the shape features reduce the size of the feature database with good precision of retrieval.

All the chapter highlights the research insights with relevant experimental results, analysis and illustration.

To sum up the book, new strategies are being devised based on Strength Matrix (SM), Tag Ranking Image Retrieval (TRIR), Geometric Margin based Shape Features of Object (GMSFO), Fuzzy Object Shape for Image Retrieval (FOSIR) and Indexing Shape Pattern combining text features with shape features for Shape Based Image Retrieval. These newly devised techniques to be a valuable addition to the domain of Multimedia Information Retrieval Systems, due to their assured performance and greater importance that qualify themselves.

KEY FEATURES OF THE BOOK

The following are the important features of the book:

- Gives a complete picture of TBIR and CBIR approches for Multimedia Information Retrieval (MIR)
- Proposes a novel conceptualisation around the ideas of Image Retrieval (IR)
- Use the text around the images in web documents for image retrival applications
- Understands the syntatical context and textual context of images in web document
- Defines margin based propertices of objects in images to capture the shape information
- Formulates FOS properties for capturing impreciseness of shape information
- Proposes a novel similarity measure for matching FOS objects

- Designs a newer pattren based indexing scheme to index large number of low level features
- Combines content based and text based pattern for imporving semantic understanding for effective CBIR applications
- Relevant for both library and information science and information technology specialists

Chapter 1
Text–Based Image Retrieval

ABSTRACT

The role of textual keywords for capturing the high-level semantics of an image in HTML document is studied. It is observed that the keywords present in HTML documents can be effectively used for describing the high-level semantics of the images appear in the same document. Techniques for processing HTML documents and Tag Ranking for Image Retrieval (TRIR) is explained for capturing semantic information about the images for retrieval applications. A retrieval system returns a large number of images for a query and hence it is difficult to display the most relevant images in top results. This chapter presents newly developed method for ranking the images in Web documents based on the properties of HTML TAGS in web documents for image retrieval from WWW.

INTRODUCTION

The technological advancements of Internet have increased the population of images, which demands effective retrieval mechanisms. Search engines have become indispensable tools for retrieving relevant images from WWW. In general, there are two flavors of retrieval namely, Text Based Image Retrieval (TBIR) and Content Based Image Retrieval (CBIR). The CBIR systems are suitable only for domain specific applications. It is also difficult to capture the semantics of images using low-level features alone and the semantic gap posed between the query image and database images remains as challenge. The extracted semantic features of the query image may not effectively match with

DOI: 10.4018/978-1-5225-3796-0.ch001

the database images. Additionally, the cost of time associated for extracting image features among large database is also very high. In a typical CBIR system, the query image is matched with database images and the retrieval set is ranked using a suitable similarity measure. The image retrieval can be broadly classified as Text-Based Image Retrieval and Content-Based Image Retrieval. Below, the functionality of each of these methods are discussed in detail with suitable example.

Text-Based Image Retrieval

The Text-Based Image Retrieval is relatively old method, where a text or sequence strings are provided as input query. Say for example, "an elephant with human riding on it". Thus, the query keyword may provide information about image name, date of adding, deleting, modifying, etc. However, the text based query ignores unexpressed feelings, emotions and conveys same meaning in an unusual way. In addition, the synonyms, hyponyms, homonyms and misspellings of the query text tend to increase the semantic gap. A typical TBIR system is depicted with various blocks for better understanding.

In the above Figure 1, the user submits text based query and is being processed by query processing unit. The stop words are removed and textual keywords are stemmed for making the query text suitable for precise search process. A suitable similarity measure is used for calculating the distance between the query and indexed text for ranking the database text and corresponding image. The indexed text-DB houses all the textual keywords based on an indexing structure (say inverted index) so that only a part of the database is searched. The indexed image-DB has all the corresponding images

Figure 1. A typical TBIR system

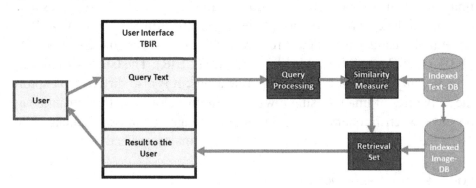

for indexed keywords. Based on the ranking, final retrieval set is processed and presented to the user is in the form of result. In conventional TBIR system, the user uses the retrieval set for his/her application as it is. However, there are advanced applications, where the users submit his/her feedback on the retrieval set with the degree of relevance to the query.

Recently, it is found that the recognition of the text present in scene image and video frames is difficult. This is due to low resolution, blur, background noise, etc. It is known that the traditional OCRs do not perform well in such images and information retrieval using keywords is considered as an alternative approach to index/retrieve such text information. Date is a useful piece of information, which has various applications, say date-wise videos/scene searching, indexing or retrieval. A date spotting algorithm based information retrieval system is available for natural scene image and video frames where text appears with complex backgrounds (Roy et al 2017). A line based date spotting approach is using Hidden Markov Model (HMM) to detect the date information in a given text. Various date models are searched from a line without segmenting characters or words. The RGB in the image is converted into gray image to enhance the text information along with other advanced methods. Similarly, the text based image retrieval is applied for retrieving Uyghur language document image dataset. The printed Uyghur document is studied and image retrieval is proposed (Batur et al 2017). The Gray scale-Gradient Co-occurrence Matrix based texture features and Hu Moment Invariant based shape features are extracted. Euclidean distance and feature distance are applied for measuring the similarity between query image and target images in the document image dataset. This method searches the relevant images without segmentation or layout analysis of document.

Mehul et al 2014, has proposed segmentation techniques to segment the text in image for medical image retrieval applications. The modern medical systems produce and stores huge amount of text, words, images and videos. Medical community requires only precise information from the large amount of stored data. However, the ICT approaches do not provide a generalized methodology for medical image retrieval and classification. Since the medical information is large, it complies with all Big Data features and constraints to retrieve relevant information.

It is found from above discussion, that medical image retrieval is tough task as big data constraints are imposed on it. As a result, suitable indexing scheme may complement the retrieval of medical images. A text based indexing system is described for mammographic images retrieval and classification. The system deals with text in the form of structured reports and image mining and classification in a typical Department of Radiology. DICOM structured reports, containing free text for medical diagnosis have been analyzed and labeled to classify the associated mammographic images. Information retrieval process is based on light semantic analysis, stop-word removal and light medical natural language processing. The system is developed with a Search Engine module using Bayes Naive Classifier (Farruggia et al 2014). Apart from indexing, the machine learning techniques such as training schemes improves the retrieval efficiency and accuracy and as a result a cross-modal regularizer is proposed (Pereira et al 2014).

Training images and text are first mapped to a common semantic space. A regularization operator is then learned for each concept in the semantic vocabulary. This operator maps the semantic descriptors of images labeled with corresponding concept to the descriptors and associated texts. A convex formulation of the learning problem is introduced to enable the efficient computation of concept-specific regularization operators. This is implemented through a quantization of the semantic space, where a regularization operator is associated with each quantization cell.

Content-Based Image Retrieval

In contrast to TBIR, the Content-Based Image Retrieval takes an image as query and searches similar images in terms of their color, texture or any other properties. Say for example, submitting a query image with "red rose" to retrieve similar images with red rose content from huge image database. Below, a typical CBIR system is presented in Figure 2.

An image is submitted as query and the feature (color, texture, shape, etc.) of the query image is extracted in the query processing unit. The similarity

Figure 2. A typical CBIR system

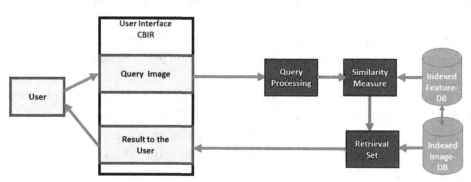

measure compares the feature of query image with the all the features in the feature database. Based on the ranking, the corresponding images in the image-DB are mapped and the retrieval set is presented to the user. It may be noted that CBIR is a process that may require long processing time due to the number of images to be compared in a database. The feature of query image is compared with all the feature in the database and a suitable similarity measure is used for calculating the distance between query and database image. The well-known similarity measures are Euclidean distance, Manhattan distance, Vector Cosine Angle distance, etc. and the similarity measure is chosen based on the applications.

A comprehensive overview on Information fusion based Content-Based Image Retrieval can be viewed in (Piras & Giacinto 2017). A convenient and precise approach for Internet image retrieval can be read from Kehua Guo et al 2016. The color is one of the well-known features of image and is represented in the form of histogram. A histogram-based image retrieval method is designed specifically for noisy query images and the images are retrieved according to histogram similarity. The histograms are described by new features which are insensitive to a Gaussian additive noise in the original images. In recent times the cloud storage is used by all the industries and individual and most of the users are concerned about the privacy of image data during Content Based Image Retrieval (Hoschl et al., 2016).

As a result, sensitive or private information in the images needs to be encrypted before outsourced to a cloud service provider. However, this causes difficulties in image retrieval and data management. A Privacy Preserving Content Based Image Retrieval method based on orthogonal decomposition is available (Xu et al., 2017). In this method the image is divided into two different components, for which encryption and feature extraction are executed separately. Thus, cloud server can extract features from an encrypted image directly and compare them with the features of the queried images, so that users can obtain the image. In contrast to other methods, this approach does not require encryption algorithms, so that it can be applied in any application domain.

In CBIR approach, the color and texture feature has been used widely by researchers and shape and object based image retrieval is used selectively based on applications. While considering shape based retrieval applications, the images are decomposed into objects and feature from each of the objects are extracted. The feature of objects can be color of the objects, texture of the objects and shape of the objects. Below in Figure 3, sample shape based retrieval is shown.

Content-Based Image Retrieval Applications

Various applications such as medicine, fingerprint identification, biodiversity information systems, digital libraries, crime prevention, historical research uses image retrieval concept and some of applications are given below for better understanding.

Medical Applications: The medical industry relies more on diagnostic images, which are produced by medical instruments. For instance, a medium-sized hospital usually performs procedures that generate medical images, which require hundreds or even thousands of gigabytes within a small space of time. It is understood that processing such huge amount of data is hard and time-consuming and thus the researchers have motivated in the field of Content-Based Image Retrieval. In fact, the medical domain is a well-known area, where Content Based Image Retrieval finds its application.

Biodiversity Information Systems: Biologists uses various types of information for biodiversity studies, including spatial data and images of living beings. The researchers have developed Biodiversity Information Systems (BIS) to perform query for understanding about species and their habitats. This is being carried out in the query by combining textual, content-based and geographical queries. For example, image of a fish

Figure 3. Sample object based retrieval (object dominant) (a) sample retrieval set (b) extracted object

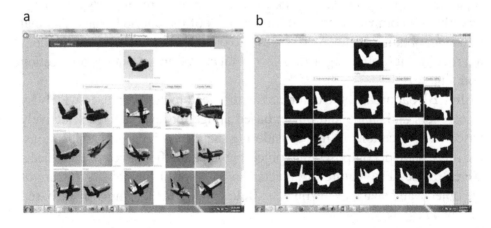

can be submitted as query with a semantic "Retrieve all database images containing fish whose fins are shaped like those of the fish in this image".

Digital Libraries: In recent times, the image content is effectively used in several digital libraries for supporting services based on image content. One example is the digital museum of butterflies, aimed at building a digital collection of Taiwanese butterflies. It is known that most of the digital library systems include a module responsible for content-based image retrieval based on color, texture, and patterns. In addition, content-based image retrieval digital library can also support geographical image retrieval. The system processes air photos that are retrieved based on texture properties. The name of the place associated with retrieved images can be attached by cross referencing with a Geographical Name Information System (GNIS) gazetter.

A BRIEF HISTORY OF TBIR

Techniques for Processing HTML Docs

In TBIR, the images are manually annotated with the text descriptions. It is well known that WWW contains a large number of images embedded in HTML documents. It is unrealistic to annotate the images manually. Moreover, designer annotations can be subjective and ambiguous. An alternative way is to consider the textual data associated with the image such as filename, caption, surrounding text and HTML TAGs for annotation. Usually, more descriptive text is available around the images and they are implicitly provided by the page designer. All these surrounded text include some form of descriptions generated by the designer about the images and is considered as a closer semantic representation. By exploiting such rich semantic textual descriptions, the TBIR has been extensively used in popular image search engines such as Google and Alta Vista. The textual data present along with HTML TAGs, such as image filename, ALT TAG can be explored for capturing the semantics. However, it is found to be difficult to select the exact feature of a web page to specifically describe the image. Those parts may not always provide hundred percent relevant text descriptions of the image that minimizes precision of search engine.

The retrieval of images from the web has received a lot of attention recently. Most of the early systems have employed text based approach, which exploits how images are structured in web documents. Sanderson and Dunlop have modeled image contents using a combination of texts from associated HTML pages (Sanderson & Dunlop, 1997). The content is modeled as a bag of words without any structure and it is considered as one of the inefficiencies of this approach for indexing. Shen et al 2000 have built chain related terms and used more information from web documents and proposed a scheme for unifying keywords with low-level visual features. The assumption made in this method is that some of the images in the database have been already annotated in terms of short phrases/keywords. These annotations are assigned either using surrounding texts of the images in HTML pages or by speech recognition or manual annotation. During retrieval, user's feedback is obtained for semantically grouping keywords with images. Color moments, Color histograms, Tamura's features, Co-occurrence matrix features and Wavelet moments are extracted for representing low-level features. An approach for unifying keywords and visual features of images (Feng et al 2001) has been proposed, in which annotations are assigned using surrounding texts of the images in HTML pages. An attempt has been made by Zhao and Grosky to improve the semantic correlation between keywords in the document title in HTML documents and image features for improving retrieval in news documents (Zhao & Grosky, 2002). Collections of 20 documents from a news site have been used and 43 keywords along with HSV based color histogram are constructed. While constructing histogram, saturation and hue axes are quantized into 10 levels to obtain H×S histogram with 100 bins. However, it is found that this technique performs well for a small number of web pages and images only. In general, image search results returned by search engine contain multiple topics and hence organizing the results into different semantic clusters would help user. A method has been proposed for analyzing the retrieval results from web search engine (Feng et al 2004) which is a bootstrapping approach to automatically annotate a large number of images from the web. It is demonstrated that the co-training approach combines the information extracted from image contents and its associated HTML text. The method VIsion-based Page Segmentation (VIPS) (Deng et al 2003) has been used to extract semantic structure of a web page based on visual presentation. The semantic structure is represented as a tree with nodes, where every node represents the degree of coherence to estimate the visual perception.

Microsoft Research Asia has developed a system for Web Image Retrieval, the purpose of which is to cluster the search results of conventional web, so that the users can find the desired images quickly. Initially, an intelligent vision based segmentation algorithm is designed to segment a web page into blocks and from the block containing image, the information related to textual and link images are extracted. Later, image graph is constructed using block-level link analysis techniques. Three types of representations are obtained for every image such as visual feature based representation, textual feature based representation and graph based representation. For each category, several images are selected as non-representative images that help the users to quickly understand the main topics of the search results. However, the time for processing tree based representation for indexing and retrieval is found to be on the higher side. Rough Set Decomposition based model has been proposed for decomposition in information retrieval (Wu and Hu, 2010) that consists of three different knowledge granules in incomplete information system. However, while WWW documents are presented along with images as input, the semantic of images are exactly captured and thus retrieval performance is low.

Tollari et al (2005) have proposed a method for mapping textual keywords with visual features of images. In order to map textual and visual information, semantic classes containing a few image samples are obtained. Each class is initialized with exactly one image and then two classes are merged based on a threshold value on distance between them. The merging process is stopped when distance between all classes are higher than the second threshold. Finally, the semantic classes are divided into two partitions as reference and test set. The reference partition provides example documents of each class, which are used to estimate the class of any image of test partition using textual, visual or combination of textual and visual information. The performance of this method is high with less number of images and corresponding textual annotations. Han et al have proposed memory learning framework for image retrieval application (Han et al 2005). This method uses a knowledge memory model for storing the semantic information by accumulating user-provided data during query interactions. The semantic relationship is predicted by applying a learning strategy among images according to the memorized knowledge. Image queries are finally performed based on seamless combination of low-level features and learned semantics. Similarly, a unified framework has also been proposed, which uses textual keywords and visual features for image retrieval applications (Feng et al 2001 & Hu et al 2000). The framework has built a set of statistical models using visual features of a small set of manually labeled images that represents semantic concepts. This semantic concept has been used for propagating keywords to unlabeled images. These models are updated regularly when more images implicitly labeled by users become available through relevance feedback. This process performs the activity of accumulation and memorization of knowledge learned from relevance feedback of users. The efficiency of relevance feedback for keyword query is improved by an entropy-based active learning strategy. An integrated patch model has been suggested by Xu and Zang (2007) which is a generative model for image categorization based on feature selection.

Feature Selection Strategy

Feature selection strategy is categorized into three steps for extracting representative feature and also to remove the noise feature. Initially, salient patches present in images are detected, clustered and keyword vocabulary is constructed. Later, the region of dominance and the salient entropy measure are calculated for reducing the non-common noises of salient patches. Categories of the images are described by an integrated patch model with the help of keywords. The textual keywords appearing in web pages are recently being used for identifying unsuitable, offensive and pornographic web sites (Hu et al 2007). In this framework, the web pages are categorized as continuous text pages, discrete text pages and image pages using decision tree with respect to their content and these pages are handled by respective classifiers. Statistical and semantic features are used for identifying pornographic nature of continuous text web pages. Similarly, Bayesian classifier and object's contour of images are being used to identify the pornographic content of discrete and image web pages respectively. Recently, the keyword is being extracted from the HTML pages and low-level features are extracted from the images present in HTML documents for retrieval applications (Vadivel et al 2009). Various low-level features have been extracted and integrated with the high-level features for relevant image retrieval. However, the association and importance of the keywords with the HTML page or with the image is not measured.

Annotation-Based Information Retrieval (ABIR)

Annotated Based Information Retrieval (ABIR) annotates each image manually using textual data and standard database management systems are employed for the retrieval task (Kiling & Alpkocak, 2011). However, annotating large image database manually is a tedious task and it is difficult to capture the semantics of the images. The low-level feature of images is replaced by the annotation for describing their semantics for retrieval purpose (Aslandogan & Yu, 1999). CBIR approach can be broadly categorized based on feature extraction as well as storing techniques (EI Kwae & Kabuka, 2000) and searching scheme (Cox et al 2000). The research direction of image retrieval is changed due to the expansion of WWW and generally the images on the web are identified with image file-name, HTML TAGs and surrounding text on the web. In the course of time, text is combined with image feature to develop the multi-model systems for improving image search results (Chen et al 2001 & Hu et al 2000). However, it is felt that combining both the low-level features and the annotation of images is a complex procedure. To overcome this, Cox et al (2000) have proposed an ABIR approach for Wikipedia pages using text data around the images. The document and query expansion schemes have been proposed using WordNet, Word Sense Disambiguation and similarity functions. However, all these expansion approaches achieve lower precision for higher recall and the explicit low-level ranking mechanism is used for improving precision. Thus, it is difficult to identify the surrounded text exactly, since the web page consists of large number of frames.

Rule-Based Low-Level Feature Analysis

Various studies have been presented to analyze textual information and are found to be suitable to describe monochromatic images. Text regions present in the image are extracted from compound document images. The region shows distinctive texture features that are different from non-text background regions (Hasan & Karam, 2000). A three-level rule-based model has been developed for image analysis. A multiplane segmentation approach for text extraction from complex document images is proposed in (Chen & Wu, 2009). Initially, these techniques have decomposed the document image into distinct object planes using multi-plane segmentation technique for extracting and separating homogenous objects. This includes, interesting textual regions, non-text objects such as graphics, pictures and background textures. Usually, this segmentation is based on the local features for processing the document images and the regions are adaptively segmented. Therefore, Chen et al. have proposed a new method that easily handles text-line, which overlaps with pictorial objects and background (Chen et al., 2012). Knowledge based text extraction and identification procedure are applied on each plane with various characteristics to detect, extract and identify text-lines. The geometric and statistical features of text-lines are encoded using knowledge rules that have established two rule sets. However, generating and extracting rules from mixed component is a time-consuming process. The images are described using the words from URL and ALT TAG for retrieval applications and the images are mapped with a predefined category. A weighted technique is proposed to extract the term based on their location in the HTML document. Normalized sum of these weights are combined with a color comparison measure by adding both values. The similar approaches with some refinement have been introduced in (Feng et al., 2001; Hu et al., 2000). A self-organizing neural network has been used by combining image features and textual information. However, it is observed that none of the above approaches have clearly mentioned the exact portion of an HTML document from where the information is extracted using scheme of combining various features.

Web-Structure-Based Approaches and Label-Based Approaches

Yanai (2003) has exploited an approach with link information and surrounding text to model an image. In addition, visual features (Gupta & Jain, 1997) are incorporated to model visual contents. The similarity between text and visual features are computed along with F1-score. Keywords in the document title of HTML page and image features are combined to improve the retrieval of news category (Zhao & Grosky, 2002). However, the semantics of images are not exactly captured while WWW documents are presented along with images as input and thus retrieval performance is low.

Various methods have also been proposed for reducing the gap between the extracted features of the systems and the user's query (Barnad & Forsyth, 2001). The semantics of the image is discovered from web pages for semantic-based image retrieval using self-organizing maps (Yang & Lee, 2006). The semantics of images is described based on the environmental text, which is surrounded by the images. The text mining process is applied by adopting self-organizing map learning algorithm as a kernel. The implicit semantic information is also discovered after the text mining process and semantic relevance measure is used for retrieval.

IMAGE INFORMATION EXTRACTION USING STRENGTH MATRIX

Why Strength Matrix?

The TBIR methods, directly or indirectly use and process the information of images in the web documents. This research study addresses this issue by proposing a feasible solution using the principle of Strength Matrix (SM) that describes the features of an image. Strength Matrix is constructed based on the Frequency of Occurrence of keywords. A large number of HTML documents (along with images) are fetched from the Internet (WWW) using a suitable web crawler. The content of HTML document, say textual keyword is extracted for capturing semantic information of images. The Frequency of Occurrence of keywords and textual information related to image URLs are used together. It is known that the image <SRC> TAG consists of sub TAGs for describing the images. Attributes such as image name, ALT Tag, optional description, etc. are used by the developer during web design.

Capturing the Relevancy of Keywords

An Internet crawler is used for crawling HTML documents along with the images. The entire scheme for fetching the document, pre-processing and other processing, etc. is depicted in Figure 4. The documents are fetched from WWW and information related to <IMG SRC> TAGs is extracted. Out of the text content, image and HTML related texts are separated out for better processing. The HTML text is pre-processed for extracting the clear text, maintaining the link between keywords and documents to understand the relationship of document and keywords. Based on these extracted information, the SM is constructed.

On the other side, the image related text is pre-processed using which the details such as caption, image name, etc. are extracted. Finally, a SM repository is constructed, which is used for retrieval applications.

The semantics of an image is described by a collection of one or more keywords. Let *I* be a set of images and *K* be a set of keywords. Assigning a keyword to an image is treated as a labeling predicate and it is written as follows.

Figure 4. The schematic diagram

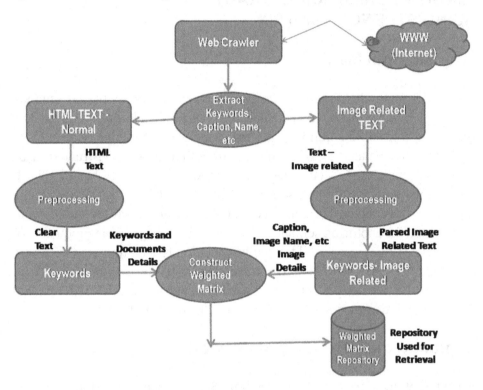

$$l : K \times I \rightarrow \left\{ True, \ False \right\} \tag{1}$$

In Equation 1, a keyword $k \in K$ can be assigned to an image $i \in I$, if $l(k,i) = True$. Since a keyword can be assigned to multiple images and multiple keywords can be assigned to one image, given a subset of keywords $K' \subseteq K$, K' can be used to define a subset of images from I as follows.

$$C_{KD}^{I}\left(K'\right) = \left\{ i \ \middle| \ i \in I \ \ and \ \ \forall k \in K', l(k,i) = True \right\} \tag{2}$$

In Equation 2, $C_{KD}^{I}\left(K'\right)$ is a set of documents with images (i) and annotated with a set of keywords K'. If we do not restrict the set of images by keyword, i.e. if $K' = \varnothing$, $C_{KD}^{I}\left(\varnothing\right) = I$, it means that all the images in the database form one set. If images could be correctly labeled by a set of K keywords, a subset $K' \subseteq K$ of keywords retrieves relevant images only resulting in 100% Recall and Precision. The main problem with a keyword-based retrieval is that it may not be feasible to manually annotate each image with keywords. It is the evident from Equation 2, that if a user specifies keywords that describe the required set of images correctly and if the relevant database images are also labeled with the same set of keywords, 100% Recall and Precision is achieved. However, due to the subjective nature of annotations, such high accuracy is not achieved in practice. Further, it would be appropriate that more high-level features of the images are to be used for capturing the semantics of the images.

Let us consider an HTML page that contains N images and M keywords and is written as,

$$K = \left\{ k_1, k_2, \ldots k_M \right\} \tag{3}$$

$$I = \left\{ i_1, i_2, \ldots i_N \right\} \tag{4}$$

It is considered that all the keywords in one HTML page are equally important and relevant to all the images in the same HTML page. The strength of the keyword k_j in the HTML document, denoted by $stg\left(k_j\right)$ is based on the Frequency of Occurrence $\left(FoC\right)$ of keyword supporting k_j

$$stg\left(k_j\right) = \left| \left\{ k_j \,\middle|\, k_j \in K \right\} \right| \Big|_{j=1\ldots M} \tag{5}$$

An association between j, k and h is captured as an expression in the form of $\left(k_j \leftrightarrow h \right)$ where k_j is a keyword $j = \left\{1\ldots.M\right\}$ in an HTML page h and is denoted by

$$stg\left(k_j \leftrightarrow h\right) = \left(\frac{stg\left(k_j\right)}{Max\left(stg\left(k_j\right)\right)} \right)_{j=1\ldots M} \tag{6}$$

Based on Equation 6, association of a set of keywords K is denoted as

$$stg\left(K,h\right) = \bigcap_{k\in K} stg\left(k,h\right) \tag{7}$$

Equation 7 denotes the association of set of keywords K to each image in belonging to HTML page h. Here, the Frequency of Occurrence $\left(FoC\right)$ of all the keywords is measured and the one with maximum value is considered for capturing the association between the keywords and images in HTML documents. The Table 1 elucidates the estimation of strength using $\left(FoC\right)$ of a keyword in a HTML document. Let the number of keywords in a HTML document is 5 and maximum $\left(FoC\right)$ is 30.

From the example in Table 1, it is observed that all keywords are not equally important. It is sufficient to consider only a set of keywords k_{stg}, in such a way that the strength of these keywords is greater than a threshold t_{stg}. In this work, a threshold is fixed as 25% of the maximum strength value. Moreover, it is important to estimate the strength of the keywords with the images. The Image Title, ALT TAG, Link Structure and Anchor Text are considered as high-level textual features and a feature vector is constructed as

$$stg\left(k_j \leftrightarrow I_{hp}\right) = stg\left(k_j \leftrightarrow h_p\right) + m\left(TAG, k_j\right) + m\left(IN, k_j\right) + m\left(LS, k_j\right) + m\left(AT, k_j\right) \tag{8}$$

Table 1. Strength matrix using Frequency of Occurrence

Keyword	(FoC)	Strength
k_1	10	0
k_2	3	1
k_3	30	1
k_4	8	0
k_5	5	1

Table 2. Strength matrix using Frequency of Occurrence and image high-level features

$Keyword$	(FoC)	$stg\left(k_j \leftrightarrow h_p\right)$	$m\ (TAG,\ k_j)$	$m\ (IN,\ k_j)$	$m\ (LS,\ k_j)$	$m\ (AT,\ k_j)$
k_1	1	0.033	1	0	0	0
k_2	30	1	1	1	1	0
k_3	20	0.66	1	0	0	1
k_4	8	0.26	1	1	1	0
k_5	5	0.16	1	0	0	1

In Equation 8, $j = 1, 2, 3, ..., q\ (q\ number\ of\ keywords)$, $m\left(TAG, k_j\right)$, $m\left(IN, k_j\right)$, $m(LS, k_j)$ and $m\left(AT, k_j\right)$ are known as match functions.

These functions match the similarity between image TAG and keyword, image name and keyword, Link Structures and keyword and Anchor Text with keyword, respectively. The output value of each function is in the range of [0-1]. This relation is effective in capturing the importance of a keyword in a document with images and it is observed that both the strength value as well as image related textual information is combined to narrow down the semantic gap of image. A sample SM with all features is depicted in Table 2.

In Table 2, k_i is a keyword extracted from HTML documents. While extracting the keywords, the stop words are removed and stemming operation is carried out. In the above example, the frequency of k_2 is high and also it matches with most of the image related textual string. As a result, k_2 have more association with the HTML page and captures the semantics of the images.

Assigning Weights to the Keywords Based on Their Position

It is observed from the previous section that the entries in SM are binary value. When k_i is equal to any of the image related textual string, value 1 is assigned otherwise 0. Also, for any k_i appearing around the images and any k_j appearing far from the image, location compared to k_i is treated equally (for

$k_i = k_j$). It is essential that both k_i and k_j should be assigned different values based on its position in the HTML document. The entire HTML page is segmented as different parts based on <IMG SRC> TAGs. In each segment, there is a set of keywords and there exists a corresponding position, which is used for assigning weights.

Let $K = \left\{ k_1, k_2, k_3 \cdots k_l \right\}$ be the keywords and $KP = \left\{ kp_1, kp_2, kp_3 \cdots kp_l \right\}$ be the position of the keywords in a segment of HTML document. While k_i of a particular segment matches with any of the textual information in <IMG SRC> TAG, more weight is assigned. Similarly, based on the physical position of a keyword, the weight is assigned. Term Weight $\left(TW \right)$ is calculated based on the probability of a keyword k_i matching with any of the TAG information and it is written as

$$TW = \Pr\left(k_i \mid ITAG\left(n \right) \right) \tag{9}$$

In Equation 9, $ITAG\left(n \right)$ is either $m\left(TAG, k_j \right)$ or $m\left(IN, k_j \right)$ or $m(AT, k_j)$. The value of *TW* depends on the *ITAG(n)*. Based on experience and analysis, the order of weights for the TAGs are $m\left(IN, k_j \right), m\left(TAG, k_j \right), m\left(AT, k_j \right)$ and $m\left(LS, k_j \right)$. For instance, if $m\left(IN, k_i \right) = true$, more weight is assigned to the keyword and for $m\left(LS, k_j \right) = true$, less weight is assigned. Thus, weights are assigned for each TAG such that the Image Name is given higher and Link State, ALT TAG are assigned lesser weight. Similarly, the keywords in a segment and corresponding distance are calculated based on its physical position. The weight of a keyword $\left(KW \right)$ is calculated using

$$KW = \left(k_i, kp_i \right) \tag{10}$$

where 'i' is the total number of keywords in a segment. The KW is the weight of a keyword with reference to its physical position from the image. Here, the reference point or position of a keyword is its physical position in a respective segment. Each keyword is referenced through a reference pointer and the distance from the reference position to the keyword is considered as its index value. Higher the index value, lower the weight for the keyword and vice versa. The final weight of a keyword $\left(FKW\right)$ for capturing semantics of an image in a segment is given as

$$FKW = KW + \left(\Pr(k_i) \mid ITAG\left(n\right)\right) \tag{11}$$

Emphasized Analysis and Performance of Strength Matrix (SM)

In order to analyze and evaluate the performance of the Strength Matrix, the Precision of retrieval and Recall is used as the measure and is given below.

$$\text{Precision} = \frac{\text{No. of Relevant Images Retrieved}}{\text{Total No. of Images Retrievd}} \tag{12}$$

$$\text{Recall} = \frac{\text{No. of Relevant Images Retrieved}}{\text{No. of Relevant Images in the Database}} \tag{13}$$

The results are compared with some of the recently proposed similar approaches and are presented in Figure 5. The average Precision (P) in percentage for 10, 20, 50 and 100 nearest neighbours is given. The performance of Strength Matrix is compared with Hierarchical Clustering (HC) (Cai et al 2004), Rough Set (RS) based approach (Wu & Hu, 2010) and Bootstrap Framework (BF) (Feng et al 2004). From the results shown in Figure 5, it is observed that the performance of Strength Matrix is quite good. The Precision of retrieval using the SM is found to be high compared to others. The reason for the performance enhancement is due to the effectiveness of SM in capturing the high level semantics of the images.

It is well known that the Precision of retrieval alone is not sufficient for measuring the retrieval performance of any method. The Recall Vs. Precision is considered as one of the important measures for evaluating the retrieval performance. However, for measuring the Recall value, it is important to have the ground truth. For each HTML pages along with images, the distinct keywords present in that page are retrieved using a suitable SQL query. This gives an idea about the distinct keywords present in a HTML page and used as ground truth information. In addition, these distinct keywords are compared with the textual information in <IMG SRC> TAG for further acquiring of ground truth information. For all these keywords, the physical position is also calculated for improving the ground truth. With the presence of the above mentioned ground truth, the Recall and Precision are calculated and is shown in Figure 6.

From the Figure 5 and 6, it is observed that the performance of Strength Matrix is encouraging compared to some of the similar recent approaches.

Figure 5. Comparison of precision of retrieval using strength matrix

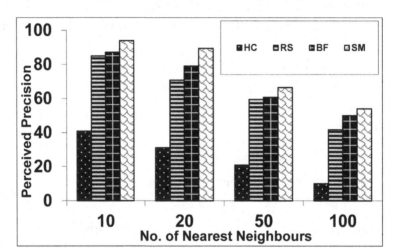

Figure 6. Comparison of recall vs. precision of retrieval

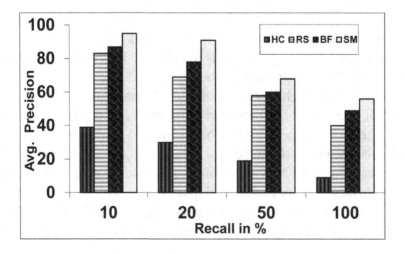

IMAGE RANKING USING IMAGE TAG ATTRIBUTES OF HTML DOCUMENTS

The researchers are constantly at their efforts in devising novel image retrieval systems, since extracting semantics of innumerable images embedded in the web pages, still remains as a challenge. This section presents principle, procedure and performance of a new image retrieval mechanism that ranking the images in the web documents using the information extracted from HTML TAGs. These ranking mechanisms use the text present in the HTML document which may not sufficient for improving the Precision of retrieval. The technique presented below analyzes the text in the <IMG SRC> TAG and each attribute in the TAG is categorized into four levels. A suitable weight is assigned to the attribute values of different levels based on the importance of each level. The top level attributes are assigned with higher weights and lower weight is assigned to the lowest level attributes.

TAG Ranking for Image Retrieval (TRIR)

This TRIR technique analyses the image TAG present in HTML documents and each attribute present within <IMG SRC> TAG is assigned a weight based on the significance of each attribute as per its hierarchy, from higher importance to lower. A suitable weight is assigned for keywords extracted from the attribute values and it is assumed that the extracted keyword captures the semantics of the image effectively.

Let us consider that a website contains a large number of HTML documents denoted as $H = \{h_1, h_2, \ldots h_p\}$. Each h_i, consists of set of <IMG SRC> TAG from which the attributes are analysed as well as the keywords are extracted and they are denoted as, $k = \{k_1, k_2, \ldots k_q\}$. Similarly, the image TAG attributes in <IMG SRC> TAG are denoted as $ITA = \{ita_1, ita_2, \ldots ita_r\}$. Let, p, q and r are the total number of HTML documents, total number of keywords and total number of attributes in <IMG SRC> TAG respectively. Usually, it is found that all the values of the attributes in <IMG SRC> TAG are assigned with suitable text by the developers, which explicitly describe the semantics of images. The keywords in each attribute can be categorized based on its characteristics and its role in describing the image content. This work employs a weighting mechanism that divides the attributes in <IMG SRC> TAGs into four distinct categories. It is known that there are approximately 24 attributes present in <IMG SRC> TAGs, by which the properties of images are described during web page design. These attributes are grouped based on their properties as Required, Optional, Standard and Event attributes. The 'SRC' and 'ALT' attributes are treated as Required attributes, align, border, etc. are considered as Optional attributes. Similarly, class, dir, etc. are considered as a Standard attributes and on abort, on click, etc. are classified as Event attributes. The properties and nature of all the attributes present within the <IMG SRC> TAG are presented briefly in Table 3.

These attributes of image TAGs are divided into four distinct levels and categorized, based on its descriptive nature and depicted in Figure 7. The Level-1 attributes are used to describe the details of the images and the keywords extracted from this level are assigned the highest weight. The title and usemap attributes are placed in Level-2 and short description about the image (i.e.) "tool tip" and the SHORT NAME of the image are extracted.

Thus, keywords extracted from these attributes gain next level of importance and weight is assigned accordingly. Similarly, the attributes in Level-3 provide general details of the image and are seldom used in <IMG SRC> TAG. Therefore, normal weight is assigned to the keywords extracted from this attribute value in Level-3. Generally, in most of the pages, no values are found for border, align, hspace, vspace, dir, width, lang, style, xml: LANG attributes and therefore they are grouped in the last level and are assigned with '1' as the weight. The values specified to the class and id attributes are so specific to the appearance of the keyword in the web page. Thus, the keywords present within these attributes assume the lowest weight. The weights for the values extracted from the attributes are calculated using Equation 14 presented below.

$$ATWGT = \sum_{LN=1}^{n} \left(\frac{(NF - TL*\text{LN})}{2 * LN} \right) \qquad where \ \ n = 1, 2, 3, ... \qquad (14)$$

where, *NF* is a Normalization Factor, which is 99, *TL* is the Total number of Levels, which is 4 and *LN* is the Level Number. Equation 14 is defined in such a way that the higher weight is assigned to the keywords present within the Level-1 TAGs and lower weight is assigned to the keywords present within the Level-2 and so on. The summed weight of a single keyword appearing only once between the TAGs of all the levels is almost 100, which means almost 100%. For instance, Equation 12 assigns weight as 48, 23 and 15 to the Level-1, Level-2 and Level-3 respectively. The keywords appearing within 'src', 'alt', 'long desc' and 'name' TAGs are assigned 48 as weight and so on.

Table 3. The properties of attribute in <IMG SRC> TAG

Required Attributes	
SRC	The URL of an image
ALT	An alternate text for an image
Optional Attributes	
ALIGN	Alignment of an image according to the surrounding element
BORDER	Width of border around image
HEIGHT	Height of image
HSPACE	White space on left and right of image
ISMAP	Server side image
LONG DESC	Specifies URL to a document that contains long description of image
USEMAP	Client side image
VSPACE	Space top and bottom of image
WIDTH	Width of image
Standard Attributes	
CLASS	Class name for the element
DIR	Text direction for content
ID	Unique id for element
LANG	Lang code for the content in an element
STYLE	Inline Style for an element
TITLE	Extra information about an element
XML:LANG	In XML document
Event Attributes	
ONABORT	Run while loading of an image is interrupted
ONCLICK	Run on mouse click
ONDBLCLICK	Run on double click
ONMOUSEDOWN	Mouse button pressed
MOUSEMOVE	Mouse pointer moves
MOUSEOUT	Mouse pointer moves out of an element
MOUSEOVER	Mouse pointer moves over an element
MOUSEUP	Mouse button in released
KEYDOWN	A key is pressed
KEYPRESS	Key is pressed and released
KEYUP	Key is released

The value of *NF* is 99 and thus the calculated weight of a keyword appearing between any TAG is a non-negative integer. The HTML documents along

Figure 7. Attribute levels of IMG TAGs

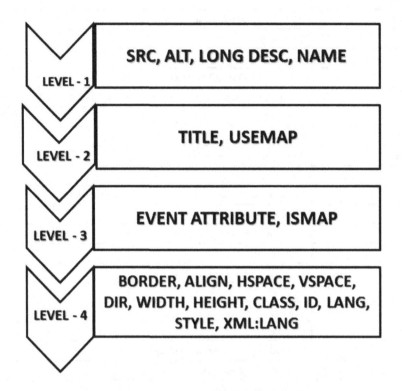

with the images are crawled. The TAGs and attributes are pre-processed, where stop words are removed and stemming is performed for capturing the properties of the images. The pre-processed keywords and the associated attributes are indexed along with the weights of the keywords. The steps followed for indexing textual keywords in<IMG SRC> TAG are illustrated with suitable examples.

The entire attributes in <IMG SRC> TAG are extracted and tokenized as keywords or terms along with attribute. The procedure for assigning weight to the keywords is explained with suitable examples. While parsing an HTML document, it is assumed that there are three <IMG SRC>TAGs and denoted as I1, I2 and I3. The TAG detail of each image is as follows.

- I1: <imgsrc="rose.jpg" alt="beautiful rose" title= "Awesome flowers" ismap="rose" />
- I2: <imgsrc="pink_rose.jpg" alt="flowers" title="Pink rose />
- I3: <imgsrc="rose.gif" class="rose" />

The attributes in I1 are tokenized as words and are pre-processed to obtain a set of keywords. In this case, 'rose.jpg' has appeared with the attribute 'src' and is represented as 'rose <->src'. The term 'beautiful' has appeared with the attribute 'alt' and is represented as 'beautiful <-> alt'. Similarly, all other terms appearing for I1 are represented as 'rose <-> alt', 'awesome <-> title', 'flowers <-> title', 'rose<->ismap'. From I2, 'pink <->src' is extracted and other terms are represented as 'rose <->src', 'flowers <-> alt', 'pink <-> title', 'rose <-> title'. Finally, 'rose <->src' and 'rose <-> class' are extracted from I3. It is observed that the keyword 'rose' appeared four times with the attributes from Level-1 in the document H1 and is denoted as $H_1: L_1\{k_1(4)\}$ with a weight value as 4 x 48 = 192. For illustration, in case of five HTML documents, each of them containing images, the relationship between the keyword TAGs and the weight is shown in Table 4. In the Table, the keywords k_1, k_2, k_3, k_4 and k_5 are rose, beautiful, awesome, flower and pink respectively and similarly, other four documents are processed. The 'docid' is the id of HTML document $\{h_1, h_2, \ldots h_x\}$ and $\{k_1, k_2, \ldots k_y\}$ are keywords. Finally, the sample keyword and level relationship are used for indexing to retrieve the relevant image from WWW.

This indexing mechanism improves the Precision of retrieval in image retrieval systems and processes the query effectively for retrieving the relevant documents. For each keyword, besides TAG weight, its Frequency of Occurrence in a HTML document is also calculated using Equation 15.

$$Wgt\left(k_g, H_g\right) = \sum_{g=1}^{n} f_g Wgt_g \tag{15}$$

where k_g is keyword present in g^{th} document, H_g is the HTML document in which k_g present, f_g is the Frequency of Occurrence of k_g and Wgt_g is the calculated TAG weight for k_g. Both the TAG weight of a keyword and its Frequency of Occurrence in that particular HTML document are used for calculating the final weight as in Equation 15, which is presented in Table 5.

The inverted index consists of four parts namely a Document Identifier, Unique Keyword, Total Attribute Weight and Total Frequency of Occurrence. For instance, in Table 5 the keyword rose (k_1) from document h_1 has occurred 7 times. i.e. four times in Level-1 TAGs, once in Level-2, Level-3 and Level-4 TAGs respectively and is represented as 1-k_1-231-7. Here, the weight of k_1 is calculated as (48+48+15+48+23+48+1) = 231, where the weights related to the attributes are substituted as L_k and it is shown in the first row of Table

25

Table 4. Relationship between keywords and levels with weights

Docid	Keywords Along With Weights and Levels	Keywords Equivalent Along With Weights and Levels
H_1	$L_1\{k_1(4), k_2(1), k_4(1), k_5(1)\}$ $L_2\{k_1(1), k_3(1), k_4(1), k_5(1)\}$ $L_3\{k_1(1)\}$ $L_4\{k_1(1)\}$	$L_1\{rose(4), beautiful(1), flower(1), pink(1)\}$ $L_2\{rose(1), awesome(1), flower(1), pink(1)\}$ $L_3\{rose(1)\}$ $L_4\{rose(1)\}$
H_2	$L_1\{k_1(8), k_4(1)\}$ $L_2\{k_1(4), k_5(2)\}$ $L_3\{k_4(2)\}$ $L_4\{k_5(6), k_2(3)\}$	$L_1\{rose(8), flower(1)\}$ $L_2\{rose(4), pink(2)\}$ $L_3\{flower(2)\}$ $L_4\{pink(6), beautiful(3)\}$
H_3	$L_1\{k_3(9), k_5(1)\}$ $L_2\{k_3(5)\}$ $L_3\{k_4(5)\}$ $L_4\{k_1(4)\}$	$L_1\{awesome(9), pink(1)\}$ $L_2\{awesome(5)\}$ $L_3\{flower(5)\}$ $L_4\{rose(4)\}$
H_4	$L_1\{k_1(6), k_4(6), k_5(1)\}$ $L_2\{k_1(5), k_4(3)\}$ $L_3\{k_3(5)\}$ $L_4\{k_4(2)\}$	$L_1\{rose(6), flower(6), pink(1)\}$ $L_2\{rose(5), flower(3)\}$ $L_3\{awesome(5)\}$ $L_4\{flower(2)\}$
H_5	$L_1\{k_2(13), k_4(2), k_5(2)\}$ $L_2\{k_4(1), k_2(4)\}$ $L_3\{k_2(5)\}$ $L_4\{k_4(2), k_5(2)\}$	$L_1\{beautiful(13), flower(2), pink(2)\}$ $L_2\{flower(1), beautiful(4)\}$ $L_3\{beautiful(5)\}$ $L_4\{flower(2), pink(2)\}$

5. Similarly, the word beautiful 'k_2' and awesome 'k_3' appear once in the attribute 'alt' and 'title' and therefore '48' and '23' are assigned as weights and substituted accordingly. While considering 'k_4' and 'k_5', the weights (23+48) =>71 and (48+23) => 71 are assigned. The weight is calculated for the rest of the keywords for other HTML documents shown in Table 4. The generated inverted index is presented in Table 5 and it contains the details of the list of pre-processed words from all documents.

Further, the posting list for each distinct keyword is found from the inverted index, where a list of documents and its corresponding keyword is extracted. For illustration, let us assume that the keyword k_1 appears in two documents as $k_1(H_1, f_1, Wgt_1)$ and $k_1(H_2, f_2, Wgt_2)$ and it denotes the occurrence of 'k_1' in H_1 and H_2 with frequencies f_1 and f_2, weights Wgt_1 and Wgt_2 respectively. The weight of k_1 in both documents is calculated using Equation 15 where 'g' represents the number of the documents in which the keywords appear. The weight of a document is calculated for generating the posting list. Let the posting list of any arbitrary word be PL $t = \{(H_1, Wgt_1), (H_2, Wgt_2)\dots (H_n, Wgt_n)\}$, where H_i is the identifier of the document that contain k and Wgt_i is the weight of the term k_i in H_i. The docid's are in the range of $i=1\dots n$, where n is the total number of documents containing the keyword k_i. The posting

Table 5.Constructed inverted index using weights for entire documents

Docid	Unique Keyword	Total Attribute Weight	Total Frequency of Occurrence
1	k_1= rose	231	7
1	k_2=beautiful	48	1
1	k_3=awesome	23	1
1	k_4=flower	71	2
1	k_5=pink	71	2
2	k_1=rose	476	12
2	k_2=beautiful	3	3
2	k_4=flower	78	3
2	k_5=pink	56	8
3	k_1=rose	4	4
3	k_3=awesome	547	14
3	k_4=flower	75	5
3	k_5=pink	48	1
4	k_1=rose	403	11
4	k_3=awesome	75	5
4	k_4=flower	359	11
4	k_5=pink	48	1
5	k_2=beautiful	791	18
5	k_4=flower	121	5
5	k_5=pink	98	4

list for the sample documents is shown in Table 6 and the keyword k_1 has occurred in four documents (H_1, H_2, H_3, and H_4) with weights 231, 476, 4 and 403 respectively. The posting list for the keyword 'k_1' of H_1 is calculated by summing up the weight and frequency of 'k_1' in H_1, i.e. (231+7) => 238. Similarly, the posting list of all the keywords in the documents is calculated by summing up the respective weight and is given in Table 6. The user expresses the required semantic concept of the image in the form of text and is captured by the posting list. This approach organizes the data as posting list and reduces the storage space and retrieval time to a certain extent.

While a query is presented, the approach checks the term in the posting list for ranking and retrieval. For instance, "Rose" as query and it is matched with the keyword in posting list and retrieves the result as k_1:$(H_1,238)(H_2,488)$ $(H_3,8)(H_4,414)$. Based on the weights of keyword 238, 488, 8, 414, the web

Table 6. Extracted posting list for sample document and images

Keywords Along With the Term	Posting List
k_1=rose	{$(H_1,238)$ $(H_2,488)$ $(H_3,8)$ $(H_4,414)$}
k_2=beautiful	{$(H_1,49)$ $(H_2,3)$ $(H_5,809)$}
k_3=awesome	{$(H_1,24)$ $(H_3,561)$ $(H_4,80)$}
k_4=flower	{$(H_1,73)$ $(H_2,81)$ $(H_3,80)$ $(H_4,370)$ $(H_5,126)$}
k_5=pink	{$(H_1,73)$ $(H_2,64)$ $(H_3,49)$ $(H_4,49)$ $(H_5,102)$}

pages are ranked. In this case, it returns the URL of the pages in the order of H_2, H_4, H_1 and H_3. If the user enters two keywords say, "Rose Flower", the weights corresponding to the keywords of respective web page are summed up and the page is ranked. The weights are obtained as:

$$H_1(238 + 73) = 311$$

$$H_2(488+81) = 569$$

$$H_3(8 + 80) = 88$$

$$H_4(414 + 370) = 784$$

$$H_5(0+126) = 126$$

and the web pages are ranked in the order of H_4, H_2, H_1, H_5 and H_3. In addition, a user can quickly get the desired image by easily expressing the query in terms of keywords. While the multiple query keywords are provided as query, various logical operations such as OR, AND, etc. can be performed for improving the Precision of retrieval.

PERFORMANCE EVALUATION OF TAG RANKING OF IMAGE RETRIEVAL (TRIR)

During July 2001, Google developed Google Image Search for searching images in the Web. In July 2010, the Google Images have reported that it has received over one billion views a day. The Google image search has indexed various categories of image and the database size is large. It is felt that it would be appropriate to consider this system to confirm the merit of the TAG based method. The performance of the TRIR is assessed with the synthetic dataset generated using Google and the ones by the developed web crawler. The crawler is constructed to fetch and save both the image and related HTML page for each query. The queries related to various domains are provided in Google Image Search and links associated to top 100 results of the given query are retrieved and processed. The same sets of links are provided as input to the crawler and a few related web pages are fetched. The related datasets consist of 25 directories and cover diverse topic of interesting domains such as Colleges, Universities, Institutes, Research Center, Flower, Famous Leaders, Newspapers, Sports, Cine field and so on. It contains 35,000 web pages with 5 GB as size, where each web page contains text/images. Using this heterogeneous collection, the performance of the TRIR is evaluated. The experiments are carried out in a computer system with the configuration of Intel (R) Xeon (R) CPU @ 2.40 GHz with 12.0GB RAM and used C# language. The TRIR is executed for the synthetic dataset and the various stages of experimental setup is presented in Figure 8.

The HTML pages are crawled along with the images from WWW and pre-processed. The textual keywords and its attributes are extracted from the <IMG SRC> TAG. The posting list is generated with term weight and 'docid'. For each query, the entry of term is matched into the posting list and the retrieval set is ranked based on the term weight.

While searching images, it is observed that the user is interested in retrieving relevant images not about its descriptions. The Google system retrieves based on the description alone. In contrast, the TRIR assigns higher weight to the HTML pages with large number of images.

The TRIR is executed for various queries and the top-20 Nearest Neighbours are retrieved for comparing performance of TRIR. From the 20 result set (HTML pages), total number of images present in each webpage is counted for both the TRIR and Google. A sample result for a query term 'Abdul Kalam' is presented in Table 7. In the Table, the first column is retrieved as a result set for the query, which is an HTML page (displayed in the form URL). The number of relevant images retrieved by each method is presented in column 2 and 3 respectively. It is also observed that the HTML document ranked higher by the TRIR approach is ranked lower by Google Image search. The performance enhancement of the TRIR is due to the weight assigned to various attributes of <IMG SRC> that has effectively captured the semantic of images. The descriptive details of the images are not considered for ranking them.

Figure 8. Various stages of TRIR

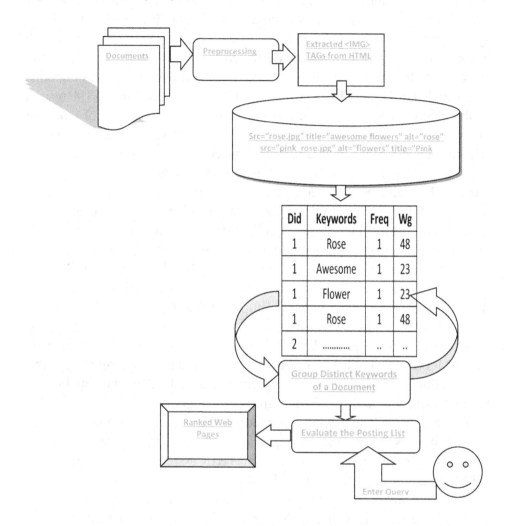

Further, the performance degradation of Google is due to the fact that it uses a page ranking mechanism. The page ranking approach gives priority to larger images, keywords around the images and keywords in file and alt TAGs. These factors have both pros and cons. One can increase the page rank of their images by using some tactics or writing a small code. Also, the user might be one among the group and higher weight is assigned to group photos. The description keyword and TAG keyword are treated equally for ranking. In contrast, the TRIR assigns weight to the keywords based on their descriptive nature and it is found that the performance of the TRIR is better.

Figure 9. Images from Top News in of A.P.J Abdul Kalam using TRIR

To further measure the performance of the TRIR, a query set is constructed by randomly selecting 150 keywords. The TRIR is compared with (Vishinu Priya & Vadivel 2012) using the same set of keywords. The comparative approach extracts the HTML TAGs along with the text present within them for the entire document from Internet for retrieval applications. The information about the whole document is extracted as well as processed that provides a description about the document and not about the images present in the WWW document. The three well-known metrics such as Precision, Recall and F1 score are used to evaluate the performance. A team having both PG students and research scholars is formed for generating the ground truth by manually extracting information from TAG's attributes. In fact, 30% of the documents are again cross checked for finally updating the ground truth information. The Precision is measured by analyzing top-100 results for every query and the average is calculated for comparing the corresponding top-100 Precision values. The Precision is calculated for the first 10, 20, 30, 40, 50, 60, 70, 80, 90 and 100 Nearest Neighbor's (images/documents) of the result set.

In Figure 10 (a), average precision for various Nearest Neighbors (NN) are shown and the comparative method is denoted as DTAG (Document TAG). For the top 10 results, average Precision of the TRIR and DTAG are 97.5% and 97% respectively. The percentage is calculated by taking the average of relevant documents in top-10 results of 150 queries. In the TRIR, the top-10 results provided for all queries are found to be relevant. For NN of 100,

Table 7. Total Number of images appeared in web page of both the systems comparative analysis of Google image vs. TRIR

Number of Images Retrieved for Query =Abdul Kalam		
Nearest Neighbour	*Google*	*TRIR*
1ˢᵗ HTML Link	*3*	*19*
2ⁿᵈ HTML Link	*19*	*5*
3ʳᵈ HTML Link	*2*	*5*
4ᵗʰ HTML Link	*1*	*8*
5ᵗʰ HTML Link	*4*	*5*
6ᵗʰ HTML Link	*5*	*1*
7ᵗʰ HTML Link	*3*	*2*
8ᵗʰ HTML Link	*1*	*3*
9ᵗʰ HTML Link	*1*	*1*
10ᵗʰ HTML Link	*1*	*5*
11ᵗʰ HTML Link	*1*	*1*
12ᵗʰ HTML Link	*2*	*2*
13ᵗʰ HTML Link	*1*	*2*
14ᵗʰ HTML Link	*1*	*2*
15ᵗʰ HTML Link	*1*	*2*
16ᵗʰ HTML Link	*1*	*4*
17ᵗʰ HTML Link	*1*	*1*
18ᵗʰ HTML Link	*1*	*1*
19ᵗʰ HTML Link	*1*	*1*
20ᵗʰ HTML Link	*5*	*1*

the TRIR and DTAG achieve 94.6% and 93% as average precision. This is because of the keywords in the randomly selected queries exist in <IMG SRC> attributes of HTML documents and the keywords related to the attributes of <IMG SRC> TAG is sufficient to describe an image semantic. In contrast, DTAG uses the description text from entire document for extracting images. In Figure 10(b), the result for Recall is provided.

The ground truth values are used to measure the recall. In Figure. 10(b), Nearest Neighbours are shown in X-axis and average Recall values are shown in the Y-axis. For each query, the average Recall is calculated using Equation 13 for all 150 queries. It is observed that while top-K pages are increased, the average Recall value decreases. In addition, the F1 score is also calculated

Figure 10. Performance Analysis of TRIR using (a) Average Precision (b) Average Recall (c) Average F1 Score

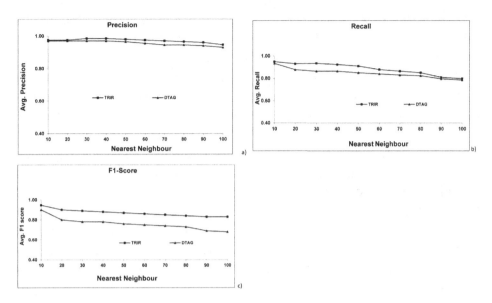

which is a measure of a test's accuracy. It considers both the Precision and the Recall of the test and is defined as. The value of F1 score is in the range of [0-1] and is depicted in Figure. 10(c). The best value of F1 score is 1 and 0 is the worst value. In the TRIR, the value of F1 score at top-10 and top-100 are 94.64% and 83.67%. Similarly, F1-score for the DTAG at top-10 and top-100 are 90% and 68%. Thus, based on all the experimental results it is observed that the performance of the TRIR is encouraging compared to DTAG and this is due to the fact that TRIR assigns a suitable weight to the keywords effectively from which the semantic description of the image is captured.

CONCLUSION

The role of textual keywords for capturing the high-level semantics of an image in HTML document is studied. It is felt that the keywords present in HTML documents can be effectively used for describing the high-level semantics of the images present in the same document. A web crawler is used to fetch the HTML document along with the images from WWW. Keywords are extracted from the HTML documents after removing stop words and performing stemming operations. The strength of each keyword is estimated and associated with HTML documents for constructing Strength Matrix. Textual information present in image URL is also extracted and combined with the Strength Matrix. Based on the text category present in the <IMG SRC> TAG, weight is assigned. The text position is also considered and weight is assigned. Both of these weights are summed and final weight is calculated.

TRIR is a hierarchical model of the TAGs in <IMG SRC> and is presented for capturing semantic information about the images for retrieval applications. A retrieval system returns a large number of images for a query and hence it is difficult to display the most relevant images in top results. The retrieval system uses a certain ranking mechanism for ranking the retrieval set such that the relevant images are ranked higher. Normally, the retrieval system considers various techniques for ranking the images such as content-based and keyword-based. Among these techniques, it is found that the keyword-based techniques effectively retrieve the relevant images. The images are retrieved using the information present in <IMG SRC> TAGs, which is used for embedding images into the web page. It is believed that the attribute values provided during the design stage of the web page capture the semantics of images exactly. Based on the importance of each attribute in TAGs, weights are assigned and the semantics are captured. The web pages are crawled from WWW with pre-processing processes such as removing stop words, stemming and other tasks. The <IMG SRC> TAG position is identified and tokenized for extracting the attribute values. These extracted values are effectively indexed for retrieval purpose. Based on the attribute level, weights are assigned and are used for ranking the retrieval set.

REFERENCES

Aslandogan, Y. A., & Yu, C. T. (1999). Techniques and Systems for Image and Video Retrieval. *IEEE Transactions on Knowledge and Data Engineering*, *11*(1), 56–63. doi:10.1109/69.755615

Barnard & Forsyth. (2001) Learning the Semantics of Words and Pictures. *Proceedings of IEEE International Conference on Computer Vision and Pattern Recognition (ICCV'01)*, *2*, 408–415.

Batur, , Tursun, Mamut, Yadikar, & Ubul. (2017). Uyghur Image Retrieval Based on SIFT Features, Procedia Computer Science. *Elseveir*, *107*, 737–742.

Cai, , He, Ma, & Wen. (2004), Hierarchical Clustering of WWW Image Search Results using Visual, Textual and Link Information. *Proceedings of the ACM International Conference on Multimedia*, 952-959. doi:10.1145/1027527.1027747

Chen, Y. L., & Wu, B. F. (2009). A multi-plane segmentation approach for text extraction from complex document images. *Pattern Recognition, 42*(7), 1419–1444. doi:10.1016/j.patcog.2008.10.032

Chen, Z., Hong, W., & Chuang, C. H. (2012). A knowledge-based system for extracting text-lines from mixed and overlapping text/graphics compound document images. *International Journal of Expert Systems with Applications, 39*(1), 494–507. doi:10.1016/j.eswa.2011.07.040

Chen, Z., Wenyin, L., Zhang, F., Li, M., & Zhang, H. (2001). Web Mining for Web Image Retrieval. *Journal of the American Society for Information Science and Technology, 52*(10), 831–839. doi:10.1002/asi.1132

Cox Ingemar, J., Miller, M. L., Minka, T. P., Papathomas, T., & Yianilos, P. N. (2000). The Bayesian Image Retrieval System, PicHunter: Theory, implementation and Psychophysical Experiments. *IEEE Transactions on Image Processing, 9*(1), 3–19. PMID:18255369

Deng Cai, Yu, Wen, & Ma. (2003). *VIPs a Vision based Page Segmentation Algorithm*. Microsoft Technical Report, MSR-TR-2003-79.

El Kwae, E. A., & Kabuka, M. R. (2000). Efficient Content-Based Indexing of Large Image Databases. *ACM Transactions on Information Systems, 18*(2), 171–210. doi:10.1145/348751.348762

Farruggia, A., Magro, R., & Vitabile, S. (2014). A text based indexing system for mammographic image retrieval and classification. *Future Generation Computer Systems, 37*, 243–251. doi:10.1016/j.future.2014.02.008

Feng, H., Shi, R., & Chua, T. S. (2004). A bootstrapping framework for annotating and retrieving WWW images. *Proceedings of 12th Annual ACM International Conference on Multimedia (MULTIMEDIA'04)*, 960-967. doi:10.1145/1027527.1027748

Feng, J., Li, M., Zhang, H.-J., & Zhang, B. (2001). A Unified Framework for Image Retrieval Using Keyword and Visual Features. *IEEE Transactions on Image Processing, 14*(7), 979–989. doi:10.1109/TIP.2005.847289 PMID:16028561

Guo, , Zhang, Zhou, Tang, & Kuang. (2016). Combined retrieval: A convenient and precise approach for Internet image retrieval Information Sciences. *Elsevier*, *358–359*, 151–163.

Gupta, A., & Jain, R. (1997). Visual Information Retrieval. *Internal Journal of Communication of ACM*, *40*(5), 70–79. doi:10.1145/253769.253798

Han, J., Ngan, K. N., Li, M., & Zhang, H. J. (2005). A Memory Learning Framework for Effective Image Retrieval. *IEEE Transactions on Image Processing*, *14*(4), 511–524. doi:10.1109/TIP.2004.841205 PMID:15825485

Hasan, Y. M. Y., & Karam, L. J. (2000). Morphological text extraction from images. *IEEE Transactions on Image Processing*, *9*(11), 1978–1983. doi:10.1109/83.877220 PMID:18262934

Höschl, C., & Flusser, J. (2016). Robust histogram-based image retrieval Pattern Recognition Letters. *Elseveir*, *69*, 72–81.

Hu, C. Z. X., Zhang, H., & Yang, Q. (2000). A Unified Framework for Semantics and Feature Based Relevance Feedback in Image Retrieval Systems. *Proceedings in Eighth ACM International Conference in Multimedia (MULTIMEDIA' 00)*, 31-37.

Hu, W., Wu, O., Chen, Z., Fu, Z., & Maybank, Z. (2007). Recognition of Pornographic Web Pages by Classifying Texts and Images. *IEEE Transactions on Pattern Analysis and Machine Intelligence*, *29*(6), 1019–1034. doi:10.1109/TPAMI.2007.1133 PMID:17431300

Kiling, D., & Alpkocak, A. (2011). An expansion and reranking approach for annotation-based image retrieval from Web. *International Journal of Expert Systems with Applications*, *38*(10), 13121–13127. doi:10.1016/j.eswa.2011.04.118

Mehul, , Ankita, Namrata, Rahul, & Sheth. (2014). Text-based Image Segmentation Methodology Open access. *Procedia Technology*, *14*, 465–472.

Pereira, J. C., & Vasconcelos, N. (2014). Cross-modal domain adaptation for text-based regularization of image semantics in image retrieval systems, Computer Vision and Image Understanding. *Elseveir*, *124*, 123–135.

Piras, L., & Giacinto, G. (2017). Information fusion in content based image retrieval: A comprehensive overview. *Information Fusion*, *37*, 50–60.

Roy, Bhunia, & Pal. (2017). Date-field retrieval in scene image and video frames using text enhancement and shape coding. *Neurocomputing*. https:// doi.org/10.1016/j.neucom.2016.08.141

Sanderson, H. M., & Dunlop, M. D. (1997). Image retrieval by hypertext links. *Proceedings of the 20th annual international ACM SIGIR conference on Research and development in information retrieval*, 296-303.

Shen, H. T., Ooi, B. C., & Tan, K. L. (2000). *Giving meaning to WWW images*. Los Angeles, CA: ACM Multimedia.

Tollari, S., Glotin, H., Le, J., & Maitre, J. L. (2005). Enhancement of Textual Images Classification using Segmented Visual Contents for Image Search Engine. *Multimedia Tools and Applications*, *25*(3), 405–417. doi:10.1007/s11042-005-6543-6

Vadivel, A., Shamik, S., & Majumdar, A. K. (2009). Image Retrieval from Web using Multiple Features Online Information Review. *Emerald*, *33*(6), 1169–1188.

Vishnu Priya, R., & Vadivel, A. (2012). *Capturing Semantics of Web Page using Weighted Tag-tree for Information Retrieval*. IGI Global.

Wu, C., & Hu, X. (2010). Applications of Rough set decompositions in Information Retrieval. *International Journal of Electrical and Electronics Engineering*, *4*(4), 285–290.

Xu, , Gong, Xiong, Xu, & Shi. (2017). A privacy-preserving content-based image retrieval method in cloud environment. *Journal of Visual Communication and Image Representation*, *43*, 164–172.

Xu, F., & Zhang, Y.-J. (2007). Integrated patch model: A Generative Model for Image Categorization based on Feature Selection. *Pattern Recognition Letters, Elsevier Science*, *28a*(12), 1581–1591. doi:10.1016/j.patrec.2007.03.016

Yanai, K. (2003). Generic image classification using visual knowledge on the web. *Proceedings of ACM Multimedia*, 167-176. doi:10.1145/957013.957047

Yang, H.-C., & Lee, C.-H. (2006). Image semantics discovery from web pages for semantic-based image retrieval using self-organizing maps. *International Journal on Expert Systems with Applications*, *34*(1), 266–279. doi:10.1016/j.eswa.2006.09.016

Zhao, R., & Grosky, W. I. (2002). Narrowing the Semantic Gap-Improved Text-Based Web Document Retrieval using Visual Features. *IEEE Transactions on Multimedia*, *4*(2), 189–200. doi:10.1109/TMM.2002.1017733

Chapter 2

Content–Based Image Retrieval Using Shape Features

ABSTRACT

This chapter presents CBIR methodologies for extracting geometric and margin features of objects in images and constructed as feature vector. This approach is unique in nature as the size of the feature is relatively small and capable of discriminating the query object with the data base object. These geometric features measure the object characteristics in terms of its shape and margin. Manhattan distance is used for measuring the similarity between query images and the database images for retrieving relevant images from the database.

INTRODUCTION

In Content Based Image Retrieval (CBIR) applications, various well-known low-level features such as color, texture and shape are extracted for describing the image semantics. It is noticed that the size of the image database for image retrieval applications is increasing exponentially and hence it is necessary to propose and use effective tools for retrieving images. The common ground for CBIR system is to extract a signature for every image based on its pixel value for comparing the images. The signature can be shape, texture, color or any other information with which two images are compared. A retrieval system retrieves both from the controlled image database and from WWW. The geometrical, margin and statistical properties of the objects present in

DOI: 10.4018/978-1-5225-3796-0.ch002

images are extracted and the feature is constructed. Shape of an image is also proved as powerful representation as it characterizes the geometry of the object. From the geometrical and margin features, the shape information is approximated and used for describing objects present in images.

BRIEF HISTORY ON CONTENT-BASED IMAGE RETRIEVAL

Colour histograms like Human Colour Perception Histogram (HCPH) (Vadivel, Shamik & Majumdhar, 2008), (Deng et al. 2001) & (Gevers & Stokman, 2004) and histograms specified in (Lu et al. 2009) as well as color-texture features like Integrated Colour and Intensity Co-occurrence Matrix (ICICM) (Vadivel, Shamik & Majumdhar, 2007) show high precision of retrieval in such applications. Similarly, other important low-level feature used for retrieval is based on shape and margin properties of the object present in images (Tran & Ono, 2003). Shape of the object is represented by a density histogram of features points (Jain & Vailaya, 1996). Based on Euclidean distance, the images are retrieved and searched by comparing the query image and the images in the database. It has been noticed that combining more low-level feature certainly improve the precision of retrieval. Both the shape and color features are combined using various strategies such as weighting (Pentland, Picard & Sclaroff, 1996), Histogram-based (Rui, She & Huang, 1998), Kernel-based (Gudivada & Raghavan, 1995) and Invariance-based (Tao & Grosky, 1999). Shape and texture using elastic energy-based approach has been proposed for measuring image similarity (Lu & Sajjanhar, 1999).

An automated color extraction and texture information using binary set representations explained in (Smith & Chang, 1996). Few research articles focus on image retrieval by segmentation found in (Freeman & Saghri, 1978). A detailed overview on the various literatures that are available on CBIR can be found in (Arkin et al. 1991) and discussion on the various similarity measurement techniques can be found in (Safar, Shababi & Sun, 2000). Though the growth of research on image retrieval is witnessed to be exponential over the past, only a very few algorithm addresses the issues related to real-time systems or applications. From the various combinations of low-level features which are tried and tested, it is noticed that they are suitable for a generic system applications. Hence, it is more relevant to build image retrieval systems that are specialized to domains. Further, the selection of appropriate features for CBIR and annotation systems remains largely ad-hoc.

CBIR Systems and Low-Level Features

Well-known and most popular image retrieval systems are QBIC, NeTra, PicToSeek, Blobworld, etc. The common ground for them is to extract a signature for every image based on its pixel value and to define a rule for comparing images. Shape of the object is represented by a density histogram of features points (Mohamed, et al. 2009). Based on Euclidean distance, the images are retrieved and searched by comparing the query image and the images in the database. It has been noticed that combining more low-level feature will certainly improve the precision of retrieval. The growth of the research on image retrieval is found to be exponential in nature. However, it appears that few of them are concerned about real-time applications or real-time systems. Various combinations of low-level features have been tried, it is noticed that a system may not cater to the needs of a generic applications. Hence, it is more relevant to build image retrieval systems that are specialized to domains. Further, the selection of appropriate features for CBIR and annotation systems remains largely ad-hoc.

Shape-Based Features

Various techniques for extracting shape features have been introduced (Yang & Lee, 2008). Edge point detection is an important step before extracting the shape and various edge detection methods have been proposed in the literature (Hou & Koh, 2003). A neural network-based shape retrieval system has been proposed for extracting the shape (Xing & Ahmed, 2009). A computational model is proposed for recognizing real world scenes without segmentation process for obtaining individual objects (Oliva & Torralba, 2001). The scene is represented as a spatial envelope with low dimension. The dominant spatial structure of science is represented in the form of a set of perceptual dimensions, which is estimated using spectral and coarsely localized information. The scenes having similarity in semantic categories are projected together in a multidimensional space. However, one of the drawbacks of this approach is that the spatial envelope properties provide only a holistic description of the scene and the local object information has not been considered. .

A method for shape recognition is introduced based on the angular analysis of Complex Networks (Scabini et al 2017). This method, model shapes as Complex Networks defining a more descriptive representation of the inner angularity of the shape's perimeter. The result is a set of measures that better describe shapes if compared to previous approaches that use only the vertices' degree. The angle between the Complex Network edges is extracted and their distribution is analyzed along with a network dynamic evolution.

The salient portion in images also attracts the most attention when people search for images in large-scale datasets. However, to improve image retrieval accuracy, considering only the most salient object in an image is insufficient because the background also influences the accuracy of image retrieval. To address this issue, Extended Salient Region (ESR) is proposed in (Zhang et al 2017). First, the salient region of an input image is detected using a Region Contrast (RC) algorithm. Then, a polar coordinate system is constructed; the centroid of the salient region is set as the pole. Next, the regions surrounding the salient region are determined by the neighboring regions, moving in a counterclockwise direction. The resulting combination of the salient region and its surrounding regions are defined as the ESR. The visual content from the ESR is extracted using the well-known Bag of Words (BoW) model based on Gabor, SIFT and HSVH features and propose a graph model of the visual content nodes to represent the input image. Then, algorithm is designed to perform matching between two images.

A Hybrid shape descriptor has proposed for shape based image retrieval (Sharma 2017). The descriptor conforms to human visual perception along with its low computational complexity. The global features are related to the holistic characteristics of images, whereas local features describe the finer details within objects of images. The hybrid descriptor uses both global and local features of images to describe the entire aspects of image shape.

Shape Feature Using Geometric and Margin Properties

The moment invariants and Zernike moments are used to construct feature vector, which describe the shape of an object (Joaquim et al 2005)). The similar images are grouped using fuzzy K-means clustering algorithm, which groups similar images and neural network has been used for retrieving similar images. One of the main drawbacks of these methods is that the fuzziness present in the objects is not captured properly and only fuzzy clustering is performed on the dataset. An MPEG-like descriptor (Zagoris, Ergina & Papamarkos, 2011) is proposed, which has both contour and region based shape features. The size of this feature is low and has a large discriminating ability. However, this approach employs a relevance feedback mechanism and it is well known that the learning algorithm takes more time to converge and may influence the retrieval time. Chahooki and Charkari (2012) has proposed region-based shape retrieval method using dissimilarities of contour and region information. Two categories of shape feature spaces are combined for improving the precision of retrieval. The multiple feature spaces are combined while constructing the shape descriptor vector as well as in decision phase. The authors have calculated dissimilarity between test and training samples using K-Nearest Neighbor (KNN) for fusion purpose. It is argued that fusion of multiple KNNs has a better shape classification accuracy compared to fuse KNN in Chicken Piece dataset. However, the performance of the method is suitable only for a subset of shapes related to chicken pieces and the accuracy is also around 90%. One of the major problems in Content Based Image Retrieval is the presence of noise in shapes, which occur in the form of continuous deformations and topological changes.

Frosini and Landi (2013) have focused on the noise, which alters the topology of the objects. The persistent Betti numbers are considered as shape descriptors that admit dissimilarity distances stable under continuous shape deformations. A general method to turn persistent Betti numbers into stable descriptors in the presence of topological changes is also presented. Retrieval tests on the Kimia-99 database, show the effectiveness of the method. Shape context based approaches have been adapted by the researchers and they have been used for processing 2D shape objects (Belongie & Malik, 2000). One of the drawbacks of shape context is that it is a time consuming process and this is due to the fact that each shape is usually described by several shape contexts (Dimo 2003). This issue has been handled and a possible solution has been proposed in (Mori, Belongie & Malik, 2001, 2005). Zhang and Lu (2002) have compared some shape descriptors that have been widely used for CBIR such as Fourier Descriptors, Grid Descriptors, Zernike moments and curvature scale space descriptors. However, these approaches have not considered robustness, compactness, computation complexity, affine invariance and ill-defined shape boundaries. Zernike moments are considered as the best method among various types of moments by considering information redundancy and noise sensibility. A major problem of noise is that it forms, continuous deformations and also changes the topological aspect of an object. A general method is presented that is able to perform even in the presence of topological changes (Frosini, 1999).

Shape- and Margin-Based Geometric Features

The objects present in the images are separated using contours information of each object and the silhouette of each object is identified and extracted. For each silhouette, the various geometric and margin properties are extracted. The shape based properties namely Area, Maximum Radius, Equivalent Diameter, Minimum Radius, Euler Number, Compactness, Elongatedness, Circularity, Eccentricity and Thinness ratio are calculated and constructed as feature vector. Each of these properties is shown below.

The area of a silhouette provides the total number of pixels present in an object of interest. The radius based properties of a silhouette is used to obtain information about the shape irregularity and is defined as MaxRadius (Mr) and MinRadius (mR). Here, Mr and mR is the maximum distance and minimum distance between the center and edge of the silhouette respectively. These measures provide the details about whether the silhouette is a regular shaped polygon or not. Euler number is a property, which provides information about the number of connected components present in a silhouette, from which the numbers of holes are identified. Equivalent Diameter *(ED)* computes the diameter of silhouette that has same area as the region, which could be used for differentiating circle and oval shape with irregular and regular shape, which is given below.

$$ED = \sqrt{\left| 4 * \frac{Area}{\pi} \right|} \tag{1}$$

The degree of deviation for silhouette from the perfect circle is extracted to form Compactness *(CN)* which is defined as

$$CN = \left| \frac{2 * \sqrt{Area * \pi}}{Perimeter} \right| \tag{2}$$

This independent linear transformation provides the degree of roughness of the region of the silhouette. While Elongatedness *(EN)* used with area, one can get the ratio of minimum dimension to maximum dimension of a rectangle shaped silhouette. It also differentiates the irregular and regular rectangle shaped silhouette and it is given as

$$EN = \left| \frac{Area}{(2 * MaxRadius)^2} \right| \tag{3}$$

Similar to above, the area with Circularity *(CT)* and Thinness Ratio *(TR)* are used to extract more circular properties and it can be used to differentiate circle and line, which are presented here in under

$$CT = \sqrt{\frac{Area}{A * Max\ Radius^2}} \tag{4}$$

$$TR = \left(\frac{4 * \pi * Area}{perimeter^2} \right) \tag{5}$$

The last shape based property is Eccentricity *(ECT)* by which the elongation is measured and it is given below

$$ECT = \sqrt{1 - \left(\frac{MinRadius}{MaxRadius} \right)^2} \tag{6}$$

The Perimeter and Circularity $\left(CT_{Mr,mR} \right)$ are extracted using radius parameters. The Dispersion *(DP)* and Shape Index *(SI)* of silhouette are extracted as margin based properties. The number of pixels in the boundary of the silhouette is the perimeter and is used for differentiating the regular shaped silhouette with irregular. The circularity shown in Equation (7), which uses the area Maximum Radius value is slightly modified, such that the ratio of minimum radius value to maximum radius value is used. The circularity ratio is used for distinguishing ellipse and circle based silhouette is computed as;

$$CT_{Mr,mR} = \sqrt{\left(\frac{MinRadius}{Maxradius} \right)} \tag{7}$$

The irregularity of a silhouette in and around the boundary is captured by Dispersion using Equation (8).

$$DP = \left(\frac{MaxRadius}{Area} \right) \tag{8}$$

The surface curvature of the silhouette provides information about the margin characteristics in which the skinny silhouette is differentiated from the regular silhouette and is given in Equation (9).

$$SI = \left(\frac{Perimeter}{2 * MaxRadius} \right) \tag{9}$$

Extracting Shape, Margin, and Statistical Properties of Silhouette

The procedure for extracting the features from the silhouette is presented in this section. Apart from the shape and margin properties, the statistical features such as Entropy of object, Standard Deviation of both silhouette and edge of the silhouette are also extracted for improving the representation of silhouette. The overall scheme of feature extraction is presented in Figure 1. In feature extraction process, the images from the databases are fetched one by one and the shape, margin and statistical features are extracted. These extracted features are linearly combined to form a single feature vector with 18 dimensions.

The contour is extracted using the Canny filter and contour is filled for obtaining final silhouette. The sample images are chosen in such a way that each of them have different shapes and thus different margins.

In Table 1, the sample geometrical and margin features extracted from the example images (shown in Figure 2) are given. The type of features is shown in the first column and the values are shown in the second, third and fourth columns respectively. All these values are extracted for entire database images and stored in the feature database. For a given query, the same values are extracted and the feature vector is constructed and it is compared with all the database images for ranking.

Figure 1. Feature extraction procedure

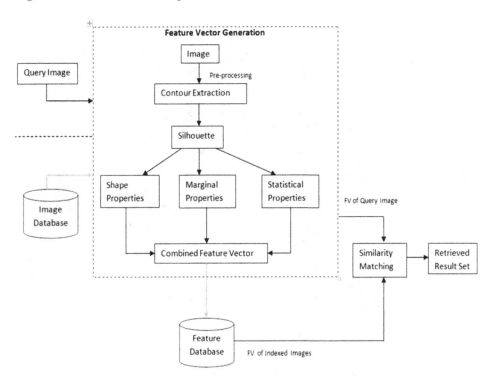

Results and Discussion

In general, the performance metrics such as Precision and Recall are the two widely used measures for evaluating the extracted results of the retrieval applications. The Precision is measured as the ratio of the number of the relevant images retrieved to the total number of images retrieved. In order to evaluate the performance of the Geometric and Margin Based Shape Feature of Objects (GMSFO), coral benchmark database images with 10 classes of different categories such as people, vehicle, building, flower, horses, etc. are considered. Ten number of query images are selected from each category and the result is retrieved for each query. The average Precision and Recall is calculated and Recall Vs. Precision is shown in the Figure 3.

It is observed from the figure that for lower values of Recall, the Precision is higher, which is greater than 65%. Similarly, for higher value of Recall, the Precision is comparable and the performance of the GMSFO is good. In addition, margin and shape based features are extracted using similar recently proposed approaches and are compared with the performance. In Table 2, the

Figure 2. Sample images from Benchmark datasets (a) original image (b) contour image (c) silhouette image

(a)   (b)   (c)

average Precision using these approaches for various combination of Nearest Neighbors (NN) is presented. The methods used for comparison are ARC-BC proposed by Zaiane et al (2002), Convexity Measures proposed by Paul (2009), SVM with Gaussian Kernel method proposed by Papadopoulosa et al

Table 1. Sample geometric and margin properties

	368.jpg	415.jpg	612.jpg
AreaPercent	0.734	0.2069	0.4721
Equiv Diameter	0.0042	0.003	0.0052
Max Radius	0.0036	0.0188	0.0059
Min Radius	0.00067163	0.0004026	0.0007691
Euler Number	1.3859E-05	4.9169E-05	2.1546E-05
Compactness	7.2183E-06	3.9203E-06	8.6278E-06
Modified Elongatedness	3.7398E-06	2.4029E-07	3.3634E-06
Modified Circularity	8.1256E-06	3.8795E-06	9.6081E-06
Modified Eccentricity	1.3613E-05	4.9158E-05	2.1361E-05
Thinness Ratio	3.7595E-06	3.1257E-07	3.4549E-06
Perimeter	0.0253	0.1169	0.0411
Modified Circularity2	6.0023E-06	7.1926E-06	7.7962E-06
Modified Dispersion	4.9697E-08	6.5737E-06	1.2657E-07
Modified Shape Index	4.8988E-05	0.00015278	7.5342E-05
Entropy	1.1582E-05	3.6164E-05	2.1498E-05

(2005), mRMR – SVM proposed by Osta, et al (2008) and Genetic Algorithm (GA) based feature selection with NN proposed by Zhang et al. (2005). While these approaches use geometrical feature in different context, these features are extracted and compared with the GMSFO in retrieval context. The reason for using these methods for comparison is that all the methods are describing the shape and margin properties of an object based on its geometrical features.

It is observed from Table 2 that the performance by ARC-BC is low compared to all other approaches. Convexity Measures, SVM with Gaussian Kernel and GA based feature selection with nearest neighbor measures exhibit similar retrieval performance. The performance of the GMSFO is good compared to all approaches. The reason for this performance enhancement is due to the fact that all the images are being considered as a combination of objects. There is no role of color and texture features. In this situation, it is required to represent the objects as understandable by human. The GMSFO

Figure 3. Average precision vs. recall

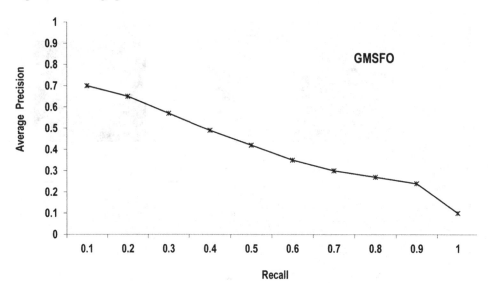

Table 2. Average precision

Method	10%	20%	50%	70%	100%
GMSFO	68.09	61.76	54.54	50.01	40.43
ARC-BC	27.59	19.32	13.5	10.0	8.9
Convexity Measures	43.00	36.91	29.98	20.01	17.23
SVM with Gaussian Kernel	40.00	34.98	31.09	26.06	20.76
mRMR – SVM	38.65	31.87	25.08	19.89	15.67
GA based feature selection with NN	41.98	37.76	31.00	26.78	20.91

represents the object and extracts the geometrical feature, which is similar to the understanding of human.

In addition to the above presented results, the benchmark datasets are also considered. Initially, LabelMe benchmark dataset (http://cvcl.mit.edu/database.htm) with 9356 images is used in which 9144 object dominant images are categorized into 101 classes and 212 texture dominant images categorized into 19 classes. Similar types of images are kept in the same folder structure. The classes are created based on certain semantic relevance among the images in a class, which is being considered as the ground truth. As a result, if an image in the retrieval set belongs to the query class, the image is considered as relevant otherwise it is irrelevant. The retrieval is performed by a group of graduate and research students for calculating the Precision of retrieval for various Recall values. In fact, the Precision values are cross checked for 10% of the queries. The group has considered 2,500 object dominated images from various categories of LabelMe data set as query images and the Mean are taken over all the 2,500 query images with ground-truth. The performance of GMSFO on LabelMe is presented below in Table 3, where the Mean Precision of retrieval is shown for different Recall values. Results are obtained for different values of Recall from 0.1 to 1.0 in steps of 0.1 and the corresponding Precision is calculated. For all the comparative methods, the proposed similarity measure is used as the distance metric. Higher the distance, the higher is the similarity between a query image and a target image. It is observed that GMSFO outperforms all the similar methods. It is noticed that the Precision of GMSFO holds during quite large values of Recall before they start to degrade. Besides having high value of Mean Precision, it is also important for image retrieval systems to have a low Standard Deviation of Precision so that the quality of retrieval appears equally good for different observers.

To study this, the Standard Deviation of Precision for all the methods is calculated and shown in Table 4. It is observed that the Standard Deviation with the GMSFO is low compared to other methods. In addition to the Mean and Standard Deviation of Precision, the Coefficient of Variation (CV) is calculated. It is defined as the ratio of the Standard Deviation to the Mean, which is the inverse of signal-to-noise ratio. It shows the extent of variability in relation to the Mean of the population. The Coefficient of Variation is computed only for data measured on a ratio scale, as these are measurements

Table 3. Recall vs. mean precision on LabelMe dataset

Method	Recall									
	0.1	0.2	0.3	0.4	0.5	0.6	0.7	0.8	0.9	1.0
GMSFO	0.95	0.94	0.92	0.90	0.88	0.85	0.84	0.83	0.80	0.74
ARC-BC	0.89	0.86	0.84	0.82	0.79	0.77	0.74	0.70	0.68	0.65
Convexity Measures	0.88	0.87	0.86	0.84	0.83	0.80	0.78	0.75	0.72	0.69
SVM with Gaussian Kernel	0.90	0.88	0.86	0.84	0.83	0.81	0.79	0.77	0.75	0.73
mRMR – SVM	0.91	0.88	0.85	0.82	0.80	0.78	0.75	0.72	0.69	0.66
GA based feature selection with NN	0.91	0.90	0.89	0.86	0.85	0.83	0.81	0.79	0.77	0.74

that can only take non-negative values. The Coefficient of Variation may not have any meaning for data on an interval scale. The Recall vs. Coefficient of Variation of Precision on a controlled database of 9356 images is presented below in Table 5 and it is observed that the performance of GMSFO is encouraging.

In addition to the results given above, the performance is evaluated on GRAZ-01 database developed by the Institute of Electrical Measurement and Measurement Signal Processing, Graz University of Technology (http://www.emt.tugraz.at/~pinz/data/GRAZ_01/) and Oxford Building Data Set (http://www.robots.ox.ac.uk/~vgg/data/oxbuildings/) developed by Visual Geometry Group, Department of Engineering Science, University of Oxford. The database consists of categories such as BIKES, PERSONS, BIKES and NO PERSONS, NO BIKES. In the bike category, four groups are maintained (image Nos. 001 to 373), four groups in person category (image Nos. 001-

Table 4. Recall vs. standard deviation of precision on LabelMe dataset

Method	Recall									
	0.1	0.2	0.3	0.4	0.5	0.6	0.7	0.8	0.9	1.0
GMSFO	0.08	0.15	0.19	0.21	0.26	0.30	0.32	0.36	0.40	0.42
ARC-BC	0.75	0.76	0.76	0.77	0.75	0.78	0.79	0.79	0.79	0.79
Convexity Measures	0.50	0.57	0.60	0.60	0.61	0.62	0.63	0.64	0.65	0.65
SVM with Gaussian Kernel	0.20	0.21	0.21	0.22	0.23	0.23	0.24	0.25	0.26	0.26
mRMR – SVM	0.18	0.20	0.21	0.21	0.22	0.22	0.23	0.25	0.25	0.25
GA based feature selection with NN	0.15	0.16	0.18	0.20	0.21	0.21	0.21	0.22	0.22	0.22

Table 5. Recall vs. coefficient of variation of precision on LabelMe dataset

Method	Recall									
	0.1	0.2	0.3	0.4	0.5	0.6	0.7	0.8	0.9	1.0
GMSFO	0.08	0.16	0.21	0.23	0.30	0.35	0.38	0.43	0.50	0.57
ARC-BC	0.84	0.88	0.90	0.94	0.95	1.01	1.07	1.13	1.16	1.22
Convexity Measures	0.57	0.66	0.70	0.71	0.73	0.78	0.81	0.85	0.90	0.94
SVM with Gaussian Kernel	0.22	0.24	0.24	0.26	0.28	0.28	0.30	0.32	0.35	0.36
mRMR – SVM	0.20	0.23	0.25	0.26	0.28	0.28	0.31	0.35	0.36	0.38
GA based feature selection with NN	0.16	0.18	0.20	0.23	0.25	0.25	0.26	0.28	0.29	0.30

Table 6. Recall vs. mean precision on GRAZ-01 dataset

Method	Recall									
	0.1	0.2	0.3	0.4	0.5	0.6	0.7	0.8	0.9	1.0
GMSFO	0.93	0.91	0.89	0.87	0.85	0.83	0.81	0.80	0.79	0.77
ARC-BC	0.90	0.87	0.85	0.81	0.79	075	0.73	0.71	0.69	0.65
Convexity Measures	0.89	0.87	0.85	0.83	0.80	0.77	0.74	0.71	0.69	0.65
SVM with Gaussian Kernel	0.88	0.86	0.85	0.83	0.81	0.80	0.78	0.77	0.75	0.72
mRMR – SVM	0.88	0.87	0.86	0.85	0.84	0.82	0.81	0.80	0.78	0.76
GA based feature selection with NN	0.89	0.88	0.87	0.86	0.85	0.83	0.82	0.81	0.80	0.78

460), four groups in persons and bike (image Nos. 001 to 210) and finally two groups in NO PERSONS and NO BIKES categories (image Nos. 001-273). The database consists of ground truth for the first 150 images belonging to bike category and it is being considered as ground truth to validate the GMFSO. In addition, the categories having images of different groups are numbered and considered as ground truth.

During retrieval, for a query image belonging to a category (group), the retrieval set is verified. In the retrieval set, if an image belongs to a query group is found, it is considered as relevant, and if otherwise, it is irrelevant. Similar to LabelMe data set, 10% of the retrieval set is verified manually by graduate and research students in our research group. The Oxford Buildings Dataset consists of 5062 images collected from Flickr (https://www.flickr.com/) by searching for particular Oxford landmarks. The collection has been manually annotated to generate a comprehensive ground truth for 11 different landmarks, each represented by 5 possible queries. The ground truth available with the dataset is considered. Moreover, the ground truth and 10% of the retrieval set are verified manually by students from our research group as it is done for other dataset.

To add, the other benchmark datasets are also considered, where the content of the images is natural scenery and the background and foreground have similar color property. The object content of the images is also very less. In Table 12, the performance evaluation of GMSFO is given on MIT saliency benchmark dataset (http://saliency.mit.edu/downloads.html). This database consists of 300 natural images and has been developed for the eye tracking problem. The relevant set is manually found using the same student group and measured the performance for 50 queries. In contrast to all the results given above, the performance of GMSFO is not good. This is due to

Table 7. Recall vs. standard deviation of precision on GRAZ-01 dataset

Method	Recall									
	0.1	**0.2**	**0.3**	**0.4**	**0.5**	**0.6**	**0.7**	**0.8**	**0.9**	**1.0**
GMSFO	0.10	0.14	0.19	0.24	0.29	0.35	0.38	0.43	0.47	0.51
ARC-BC	0.88	0.95	1.00	1.10	1.19	0.01	1.29	1.34	1.39	1.49
Convexity Measures	0.73	0.77	0.84	0.88	0.93	0.97	1.04	1.10	1.14	1.23
SVM with Gaussian Kernel	0.40	0.42	0.45	0.48	0.51	0.51	0.54	0.56	0.59	0.63
mRMR – SVM	0.34	0.37	0.38	0.41	0.44	0.46	0.48	0.49	0.51	0.54
GA based feature selection with NN	0.31	0.32	0.32	0.34	0.35	0.37	0.39	0.42	0.44	0.46

Table 8. Recall vs. coefficient of variation of precision on GRAZ-01 dataset

Method	Recall									
	0.1	**0.2**	**0.3**	**0.4**	**0.5**	**0.6**	**0.7**	**0.8**	**0.9**	**1.0**
GMSFO	0.06	0.08	0.09	0.12	0.14	0.17	0.18	0.21	0.23	0.24
ARC-BC	0.76	0.8	0.83	0.87	0.92	0.95	0.98	1.03	1.06	1.1
Convexity Measures	0.6	0.63	0.69	0.72	0.74	0.76	0.81	0.84	0.86	0.93
SVM with Gaussian Kernel	0.27	0.29	0.31	0.34	0.36	0.37	0.39	0.41	0.43	0.47
mRMR – SVM	0.22	0.24	0.26	0.28	0.31	0.32	0.34	0.35	0.38	0.41
GA based feature selection with NN	0.19	0.19	0.19	0.21	0.22	0.25	0.27	0.3	0.31	0.33

Table 9. Recall vs. mean precision on Oxford Building dataset

Method	Recall									
	0.1	**0.2**	**0.3**	**0.4**	**0.5**	**0.6**	**0.7**	**0.8**	**0.9**	**1.0**
GMSFO	0.96	0.95	0.93	0.91	0.90	0.89	0.87	0.85	0.84	0.82
ARC-BC	0.85	0.84	0.83	0.82	0.81	0.80	0.79	0.78	0.77	0.76
Convexity Measures	0.86	0.85	0.83	0.81	0.80	0.78	0.77	0.76	0.75	0.74
SVM with Gaussian Kernel	0.87	0.86	0.85	0.83	0.81	0.80	0.78	0.76	0.75	0.73
mRMR – SVM	0.88	0.86	0.85	0.83	0.81	0.80	0.78	0.76	0.76	0.75
GA based feature selection with NN	0.90	0.89	0.87	0.86	0.85	0.83	0.81	0.80	0.79	0.78

Table 10. Recall vs. standard deviation of precision on Oxford Building dataset

Method	Recall									
	0.1	0.2	0.3	0.4	0.5	0.6	0.7	0.8	0.9	1.0
GMSFO	0.15	0.19	0.22	0.25	0.28	0.30	0.32	0.33	0.35	0.36
ARC-BC	0.76	0.77	0.79	0.81	0.84	0.85	0.86	0.87	0.87	0.88
Convexity Measures	0.76	0.77	0.78	0.79	0.81	0.82	0.82	0.83	0.83	0.84
SVM with Gaussian Kernel	0.41	0.43	0.45	0.46	0.47	0.48	0.50	0.52	0.53	0.54
mRMR – SVM	0.40	0.43	0.43	0.45	0.47	0.48	0.49	0.50	0.51	0.52
GA based feature selection with NN	0.32	0.33	0.34	0.36	0.38	0.38	0.39	0.40	0.41	0.43

Table 11. Recall vs. coefficient of variation of precision on Oxford Building dataset

Method	Recall									
	0.1	0.2	0.3	0.4	0.5	0.6	0.7	0.8	0.9	1.0
GMSFO	0.16	0.20	0.24	0.27	0.31	0.34	0.37	0.39	0.42	0.44
ARC-BC	0.89	0.92	0.95	0.99	1.04	1.06	1.09	1.12	1.13	1.16
Convexity Measures	0.88	0.91	0.94	0.98	1.01	1.05	1.06	1.09	1.11	1.14
SVM with Gaussian Kernel	0.47	0.50	0.53	0.55	0.58	0.60	0.64	0.68	0.71	0.74
mRMR – SVM	0.45	0.50	0.51	0.54	0.58	0.60	0.63	0.66	0.67	0.69
GA based feature selection with NN	0.36	0.37	0.39	0.42	0.45	0.46	0.48	0.50	0.52	0.55

the fact that the images of natural scenery are not object dominant and as a result, poses difficulties while separating different objects present in images. However, the performance of the GMSFO is encouraging compared to other similar approaches. Also, the image collection of the IAPR TC-12 Benchmark dataset (http://imageclef.org/photodata) with 20,000 still natural images is taken from locations around the world to comprise an assorted cross-section of still natural images.

This includes pictures of different sports and actions, photographs of people, animals, cities, landscapes and many other aspects of contemporary life. Each image is associated with a text caption in English, German and Spanish. These annotations are stored in a database, which is managed by a benchmark administration system that allows the specification of parameters according to which different subsets of the image collection can be generated. The ground truth for this result is generated by the group of students based

Table 12. Recall vs. mean precision on MIT Saliency dataset

Method	Recall									
	0.1	0.2	0.3	0.4	0.5	0.6	0.7	0.8	0.9	1.0
GMSFO	0.80	0.79	0.77	0.75	0.73	0.72	0.74	0.70	0.67	0.64
ARC-BC	0.75	0.73	0.71	0.68	0.65	0.65	0.61	0.59	0.57	0.54
Convexity Measures	0.75	0.74	0.73	0.71	0.69	0.68	0.67	0.66	0.64	0.61
SVM with Gaussian Kernel	0.62	0.61	0.60	0.58	0.56	0.55	0.52	0.50	0.49	0.48
mRMR – SVM	0.68	0.67	0.65	0.64	0.63	0.61	0.61	0.59	0.58	0.57
GA based feature selection with NN	0.77	0.76	0.74	0.72	0.70	0.69	0.67	0.65	0.63	0.60

on the annotations available in the dataset and the Precision vs. Recall is calculated for 100 query images from different categories.

Below, the image database from the University of Washington (http://imagedatabase.cs.washington.edu/groundtruth/) is used for evaluating the performance. There are 23 classes, stored in a directory structure with a directory name as the image category name. For measuring the ground truth, the directory name is being used by the student group that performed the evaluation. The results are shown in Table 14. Based on the results presented in Table 2 - 14, using various controlled databases, it is noticed that the GMSFO outperforms all the other similar approaches. This is due to the fact that most of the images contain object level information, which can be used as feature for discriminating one from another.

Table 13. Recall vs. mean precision on IAPR TC-12 dataset

Method	Recall									
	0.1	0.2	0.3	0.4	0.5	0.6	0.7	0.8	0.9	1.0
GMSFO	0.89	0.87	0.85	0.83	0.81	0.79	0.77	0.75	0.73	0.71
ARC-BC	0.88	0.85	0.83	0.81	0.79	0.77	0.75	0.71	0.68	0.65
Convexity Measures	0.87	0.85	0.84	0.82	0.80	0.78	0.75	0.74	0.72	0.69
SVM with Gaussian Kernel	0.85	0.84	0.82	0.80	0.78	0.77	0.74	0.70	0.67	0.64
mRMR – SVM	0.86	0.84	0.82	0.79	0.76	0.74	0.72	0.69	0.66	0.64
GA based feature selection with NN	0.88	0.86	0.84	0.82	0.80	0.77	0.74	0.73	0.70	0.68

Table 14. Recall vs. mean precision on UW dataset

Method	Recall									
	0.1	0.2	0.3	0.4	0.5	0.6	0.7	0.8	0.9	1.0
GMSFO	0.80	0.79	0.77	0.74	0.73	0.72	0.71	0.70	0.69	0.68
ARC-BC	0.75	0.74	0.73	0.71	0.70	0.67	0.64	0.62	0.61	0.59
Convexity Measures	0.75	0.73	0.71	0.70	0.69	0.67	0.64	0.64	0.61	0.58
SVM with Gaussian Kernel	0.69	0.68	0.65	0.64	0.62	0.60	0.59	0.58	0.56	0.54
mRMR – SVM	0.75	0.73	0.71	0.69	0.67	0.65	0.63	0.61	0.60	0.59
GA based feature selection with NN	0.78	0.76	0.74	0.72	0.70	0.68	0.66	0.64	0.62	0.60

CONCLUSION

In this chapter, GMFSO is proposed for CBIR applications using geometric properties of objects present in images. These geometric features measure the object characteristics in terms of its shape and margin. Manhattan distance is used for measuring the similarity between query images and the database images for retrieving relevant images from the database. The shape and margin based properties are extracted for each and every objects in an image. Similarly, for each object feature vector is constructed and thus the feature dimension is variable. The experiments are performed using both benchmark and uncontrolled data set. The performance is evaluated using Precision and Recall. It is found that GMFSO performs well. However, the drawback of this approach is that the impreciseness and the ambiguity present in the boundary of the objects are not addressed. In the next chapter, this issue is addressed by capturing fuzzy imprecise information present in the geometric and boundary properties of objects. Suitable fuzzy membership function is used for capturing the impreciseness.

REFERENCES

Arkin, E. M., Chew, L., Huttenlocher, D., Kedem, K., & Mitchell, J. (1991). An Efficiently Computable Metric for Comparing Polygonal Shapes. *IEEE Transactions on Pattern Analysis and Machine Intelligence*, *13*(3), 209–216. doi:10.1109/34.75509

Belongie, S., & Malik, J. (2000). Matching with Shape Contexts. *Proceeding of IEEE Workshop on Content based Access of Image and Video Libraries*, 20–26. doi:10.1109/IVL.2000.853834

Chahooki, M. A. Z., & Charkari, N. M. (2012). Supervised Shape Retrieval based on Fusion of Multiple Feature Spaces. *Proceedings of 20th Iranian Conference on Electrical Engineering (ICEE'12)*, 1072-1074. doi:10.1109/IranianCEE.2012.6292512

Deng, Y. (2001). An efficient colour representation for image retrieval. *IEEE Transactions on Image Processing*, *10*(1), 140–147. doi:10.1109/83.892450 PMID:18249604

Dimo, D. (2003). Fast Shape based Image Retrieval. *Proceedings of Computer Systems and Technologies - CompSysTech E-Learning*, 296–302.

Freeman, H., & Saghri. (1978). Generalized chain codes for planar curves. *Proceedings of the 4th International Joint Conference on Pattern Recognition*, 701-703.

Frosini, P., & Landi, C. (1999). Size theory as a topological tool for computer vision. *Pattern Recognition and Image Analysis*, *9*(4), 596–603.

Frosini, P., & Landi, C. (2013). Persistent Betti numbers for a noise tolerant shape based approach to image retrieval. *Pattern Recognition Letters*, *34*(8), 863–872. doi:10.1016/j.patrec.2012.10.015

Gevers, T., & Stokman, H. M. G. (2004). Robust Histogram Construction from Color Invariants for Object Recognition. *IEEE Transactions on Pattern Analysis and Machine Intelligence*, *26*(1), 113–118. doi:10.1109/TPAMI.2004.1261083 PMID:15382690

Gudivada, V. N., & Raghavan, V. V. (1995). Special Issue on Content-Based Image Retrieval Systems. *IEEE Computer*, *28*(9), 18–22. doi:10.1109/2.410145

Hou, Z., & Koh, T. S. (2003). Robust edge detection. *Pattern Recognition, Elsevier Science*, *36*(9), 2083–2091. doi:10.1016/S0031-3203(03)00046-3

Jain, A. K., & Vailaya, A. (1996). Image retrieval using colour and shape. *Pattern Recognition, Elsevier*, *29*(8), 1233–1244. doi:10.1016/0031-3203(95)00160-3

Joaquim, C. F., Marcela, X. R., Elaine, P. M., Agma, J. M., & Caetano, T. J. (2005). A Low-cost Approach for Effective Shape-based Retrieval and Classification of Medical Images. *Proceedings of Seventh IEEE International Symposium on Multimedia (ISM'05)*, 565-570.

Lu, Yang, Zhang, & Yu. (2009) Image classification based on pyramid histogram of topics. *Proceedings of IEEE International Conference on Multimedia and Expo (ICME 2009)*, 398-401. doi:10.1109/ICME.2009.5202518

Lu, G., & Sajjanhar, A. (1999). Region-based Shape representation and Similarity Measure Suitable for Content-based Image Retrieval. *Multimedia Systems, Springer-Verlag, 7*(2), 165–174. doi:10.1007/s005300050119

Mohamed, A., Khellfi, F., Weng, Y., Jiang, J., & Ipson, S. (2009). An efficient Image Retrieval through DCT Histogram Quantization. *Proceedings of International Conference on Cyber Worlds*, 237-240. doi:10.1109/CW.2009.61

Mori, G., Belongie, S., & Malik, J. (2001). Shape contexts enable efficient retrieval of similar shapes. *Proceedings of IEEE Computer Society Conference on Computer Vision and Pattern Recognition (CVPR), 1*, 723–730. doi:10.1109/CVPR.2001.990547

Mori, G., Belongie, S., & Malik, J. (2005). Efficient shape matching using shape context. *IEEE Transactions on Pattern Analysis and Machine Intelligence, 27*(11), 1832–1837. doi:10.1109/TPAMI.2005.220 PMID:16285381

Oliva, A., & Torralba, A. (2001). Modeling the Shape of the Scene: A Holistic Representation of the Spatial Envelope. *International Journal of Computer Vision, 42*(3), 145–175. doi:10.1023/A:1011139631724

Osta, H., Qahwajiand, R., & Ipson, S. (2008). Comparisons of feature selection methods using discrete wavelet transforms and Support Vector Machines for mammogram images. *Proceedings of 5th International Multi-Conference on Systems, Signals and Devices*, 1-6.

Papadopoulosa, A., Fotiadisb, D. I., & Likas, A. (2005). Characterization of clustered microcalcifications in digitized mammograms using neural networks and support vector machines. *Artificial Intelligence in Medicine, 34*(2), 141–150. doi:10.1016/j.artmed.2004.10.001 PMID:15894178

Paul, L. (2009). Classification of pathological shapes using convexity measures. *Pattern Recognition Letters, 30*(5), 570–578. doi:10.1016/j.patrec.2008.12.001

Pentland, A., Picard, R. W., & Sclaroff, S. (1996). Photobook: Tools for content-based manipulation of image databases, Multimedia Tools and Applications. *The Kluwer International Series in Engineering and Computer Science, 359*, 43–80. doi:10.1007/978-1-4613-1387-8_2

Rui, Y., She, A. C., & Huang, T. S. (1998). Modified Fourier Descriptor for Shape Matching in MARS. Proceedings of Image Databases and Multimedia Search, 8, 165-180. doi:10.1142/9789812797988_0014

Safar, J., Shababi, C., & Sun, X. (2000). Image Retrieval by Shape: A comparative Study. *Proceedings of IEEE International Conference on Multimedia and Expo, 1*, 141-144. doi:10.1109/ICME.2000.869564

Scabini, L. F. S., Fistarol, D. O., Cantero, S. V., Gonçalves, W. N., & Rodrigues, J. F. Jr. (2017). Angular descriptors of complex networks: A novel approach for boundary shape analysis. *Expert Systems with Applications, 89*, 362–373.

Sharma, P. (2017). Improved *shape* matching and *retrieval* using robust histograms of spatially distributed points and angular radial transform. *International Journal for Light and Electron Optics, 145*, 346–364.

Smith, J. R., & Chang, S. F. (1996). Visual SEEK: A fully automated content-based image query system. *Proceedings of the Forth ACM International Conference on Multimedia (ACM MM'96)*, 87–98. doi:10.1145/244130.244151

Tao, Y., & Grosky, W. I. (1999). Delaunay Triangulation for Image Object Indexing: A Novel Method for Shape Representation. *Proceedings of IS&T/SPIE's Symposium on Storage and Retrieval for Image and Video Databases VII.*

Tran, & Ono. (2003). *Content-Based Image Retrieval: Object Representation by the Density of Feature Points.* National Institute of Informatics.

Vadivel, A., Shamik, S., & Majumdar, A. K. (2008). Robust Histogram Generation from the HSV Color Space based on Visual Perception. *International Journal on Signals and Imaging Systems Engineering, 1*(3/4), 245–254.

Vadivel, A., Sural, S., & Majumdar, A. K. (2007). An Integrated Color and Intensity Co-occurrence Matrix. *An Integrated Color and Intensity Co-Occurrence Matrix, Pattern Recognition Letters, Elsevier Science, 28*(8), 974–983. doi:10.1016/j.patrec.2007.01.004

Xing, N., & Ahmad, I. S. (2009). Shape-Based Image Retrieval. *Proceedings of 7th International Conference on Advances in Mobile Computing and Multimedia*, 545-549.

Yang, H. C., & Lee, C. H. (2008). Image Semantics Discovery from Web Pages for Semantic-based Image Retrieval using Self-organizing maps. *Expert Systems with Applications: An Integrated Journal, 34*(1), 266–279. doi:10.1016/j.eswa.2006.09.016

Zagoris, K., Ergina, K., & Papamarkos, N. (2011). Image retrieval systems based on compact shape descriptor and relevance feedback information. *Journal of Visual Communication and Image Representation, Elsevier Science, 22*(5), 378–390. doi:10.1016/j.jvcir.2011.03.002

Zaiane, O., Maria-Luiz, A., & Alexandru, C. (2002). Mammography classification by an association rule-based classifier. *Proceedings of the Third International Workshop on Multimedia Data Mining*, 62-69.

Zhang, , Feng, Li, Gao, & Yuan. (2017). Image retrieval using the extended salient region. *Information Sciences, 399*, 154–182.

Zhang, D., & Lu, G. (2002). Shape-based image retrieval using generic Fourier descriptor. *Signal Processing Image Communication, 17*(10), 825–848. doi:10.1016/S0923-5965(02)00084-X

Zhang, P., Verma, B., & Kumar, K. (2005). Neural Vs. statistical classifier in conjunction with genetic algorithm based feature selection. *Pattern Recognition, Elsevier, 26*(7), 909–919. doi:10.1016/j.patrec.2004.09.053

Chapter 3
Fuzzy Object Shape
for Image Retrieval

ABSTRACT

Compared to color and texture, the shape is considered as an important feature for many real-time applications. In this chapter, Fuzzy Object Shape (FOS) is presented for extracting the shape information present in the images. It is further noticed that the boundary of the object is ill-defined and there is impreciseness and vagueness in the object information. The closeness of the object with well-known primitive shapes are estimated. It is known that the impreciseness can be effectively captured by fuzzy functions and FOS has offered seven fuzzy membership function for the same. The value of each fuzzy membership function are constructed as feature vector to define the properties of individual objects.

INTRODUCTION

In shape based retrieval, representing shape, similarity measure and indexing are considered as the most important issues and among them the shape representation is a challenging task. Various techniques have been proposed for representing the shapes and they are broadly classified as contour-based and region-based. While the contour based approach extracts the border information of the object shape, the region-based approach considers the internal details of the shape of the object. Compared to color and texture, the contour based shape is found to play an important role in image retrieval

DOI: 10.4018/978-1-5225-3796-0.ch003

systems (Belongie, Malik & Puzicha, 2002). The region based methods, use moment descriptors to describe shape. Contour based shape representation only exploits shape boundary information and they are classified as global shape descriptors, shape signatures and spectral descriptors. Methods such as curvature scale space (Abbasi, Mokhtarian & Kittler, 1999) and (Mokhtarian & Mackworth, 1992) and Fourier descriptors (EI-ghazal, Basir and Belkasim, 2007) have been proposed for shape similarity assessment and shape retrieval. The shape geometry features, such as circularity, eccentricity and moments have been extracted for representing the shape (Flickner et al, 1995). Structural methods (Latecki & Lakamper, 2000) represent shapes as various disjoint parts with their relationships by making use of the data structures such as trees, graphs and strings.

All these shape based features describe the shape properties and ignores the impreciseness and vagueness present in the shape of the object. The impreciseness may be captured by using fuzzy logic approach (Colombo, Bimbo & Pala, 1999) and have advocated a syntactic construction of a compositional semantics to build the semantic representation of images. A Linguistic Expression Based Image Description (LEBID), which is a fuzzy semantics description framework has been proposed to validate its feasibility in texture image retrieval (Li, Luo & Shi, 1999). It is noticed that prior knowledge is required to describe the image and fuzzy rules.

A CBIR system is proposed for general purpose as well as face image databases using two MPEG-7 image descriptors. Several sophisticated fuzzy-rough feature selection methods are used and combines the results of these methods to obtain a prominent feature subset for image representation for a particular query (Islam et al 2017). Fuzzy-rough upper approximation possibly adds more similar images in the relevant list from boundary region to expand the relevant list. There is a need for profile based information seeking and retrieval systems and these systems should be able to support users with their context-aware information needs. Enterprise information seeking and retrieval systems using fuzzy logic is available to user along with document profiles to model user information seeking behavior (Alhabashneh et al 2017).

It is known from above discussion that the objects present in an image are important contents and can be used in CBIR applications. Identifying and representing the shape of the object is indeed quite complex due to the uncertainties in the boundary of an object of interest. In this chapter, Fuzzy-Object-Shape is discussed to capture the shape of the object of interest along with the degree of impreciseness in the boundary information. The Fuzzy-Object-Shape information is extracted from an image that provides the similarity measure of the object(s) of interest, in comparison with the Euclidian space objects, such as square, circle, etc. For each object, the fuzzy membership values are calculated and feature vector is constructed using these values.

FUZZY OBJECT SHAPE FOR IMAGE RETRIEVAL (FOSIR)

A very few attempts have been made to estimate the shape of an object for image retrieval applications. The performance of the fuzzy system is proved to be better than the traditional systems since it has the ability to deal with the uncertainties. Estimating the shape of an object is considered as a complex task when its margin is irregular. Based on the contour and region information, the object of interest present in the image is identified and its silhouette is extracted. The background idea of FOSIR and the similarity measure is presented in the next section.

Background of FOSIR

In the Chapter 2, the shape and margin characteristics of objects present in images are extracted using geometric features and the feature vector is constructed. The shape based properties such as Area, Maximum Radius, Equivalent Diameter, Minimum Radius, Euler Number, Compactness, Elongatedness, Circularity, Eccentricity and Thinness Ratio are used for discriminating one object from another. These properties are derived using Minimum and Maximum radius either directly or indirectly. These properties can be used for discriminating between the regular object and the irregular object. The geometric and margin properties derived using Minimum and Maximum radius is presented in Table 1.

These properties are calculated for each object and constructed as a feature vector. This feature vector provides information about the shape of the objects. However, the boundaries of most of the objects are irregular and they cannot be marked exactly. This leads to vagueness and impreciseness and the feature may not accurately capture the shape information of an object. The fuzzy based membership function for the primitive shapes, forms the baseline for Fuzzy Object Shape for Image Retrieval (FOSIR).

Table 1. The shape and margin based properties of objects

S.No.	Property	Explanation
	Area Based Properties	
1	$ED = \sqrt{4 * \left(\dfrac{Area}{\pi} \right)}$	Equivalent Diameter *(ED)* computes the diameter of silhouette that has the same area as the region, which could be used for differentiating between the circle and oval shape with irregular and regular shape. Here, the Area is the size of an object and is measured as the number of pixels contributing to the object.
2	$CN = \left\| \dfrac{2 * \sqrt{Area * \pi}}{Perimeter} \right\|$	Compactness *(CN)* provides the degree of deviation of an object from the perfect circle. Here, the Perimeter is the total number of pixels in the boundary of an object.
3	$EN = \left(\dfrac{Area}{\left(2 * Mr\right)^2} \right)$	Elongatedness *(EN)* provides the degree of roughness and is independent of linear transformations of the object. The regular and irregular property of the rectangle can be differentiated effectively. Here, *Mr* is the Maximum Radius of the object.
4	$CT = \sqrt{\dfrac{Area}{\left(\pi * Mr\right)^2}}$	Circularity *(CT)* and Thinness Ratio *(TR)* are used to extract more circular properties which are used to discriminate circle and line.
5	$TR = \left(\dfrac{4 * \pi * Area}{Perimeter^2} \right)$	
6	$ECT = \sqrt{1 - \left(\dfrac{mR}{Mr} \right)^2}$	Elongation of an object is measured by Eccentricity *(ECT)*. Here *mR* is the Minimum Radius of the object.
	Margin Based Properties	
7	$CT_{Mr,mR} = \sqrt{\left(\dfrac{mR}{Mr} \right)}$	Circularity *(CT)* ratio is used to distinguish the ellipse and circular property of an object.
8	$DP = \dfrac{Mr}{Area}$	Dispersion *(DP)* captures the irregularity of a shape around the boundary of an object
9	$SI = \left(\dfrac{Perimeter}{2 * Mr} \right)$	Shape Index *(SI)* provides information about the surface curvature of an object, which is about the margin characteristics to differentiate skinny shape from the regular shape of an object.

Fuzzy-Based Membership Function for Primitive Shapes

The radius properties of the object are used for obtaining information about the shape irregularity. *Mr* and *mR* are the maximum and minimum length that bisects the diagonal in each of the primitive shapes. For the sake of convenience and better understanding, in the rest of the chapter, *mR* and *Mr* are considered as the minimum radius *(mR)* and maximum radius *(Mr)* of the object. The minimum and maximum radius are measured from the center of the object. It is the centroid from which the distance to the boundary is measured with certain angular displacement. Among the measured samples, minimum and maximum value are considered as minimum and maximum radius.

It is well known that while $Mr/mR \to 1$, the object is a perfect circle. However, for an object with irregular boundaries, the fuzzy membership function can be defined as follows.

$$\mu_C\left(x\right) = e^{\left\{-\left(x_c - 1\right)^2\right\}} \tag{1}$$

In the above equation, $\mu_C\left(x\right)$ is the membership function defined on circles *C* and $x_c = \left(Mr + mR\right)/\left(d1 + d2\right)$ is the parameter assigned to each circle *(x)*, where *Mr* is the length, *mR* is the breadth, *d1* and *d2* are the lengths calculated diagonally. The *d1* and *d2* are used to distinguish the circle from the square. The logical representation of the circle along with the required parameters is depicted in Figure 1. It is known that the value range of Equation 1 is [0, 1] and for a perfect circle the value is 1.

The fuzzy membership function of an ellipse using minimum and maximum radius is given in Equation 2, as

$$\mu_{EL}\left(x\right) = e^{\left\{-x_{el} - 1\right\}} \tag{2}$$

Unlike circle, the ellipse has different lengths of diameter based on the orientation, where $\mu_{EL}\left(x\right)$ denotes the membership function defined on ellipses *EL* and $x_{el} = \left(\dfrac{d1 - d2}{Mr - mR}\right) + \left(\dfrac{\angle a1}{\angle a2}\right)$ is the parameter assigned to each ellipse *(x)*.

Figure 1. The Logical Representation of Circle using Minimum and Maximum Radius

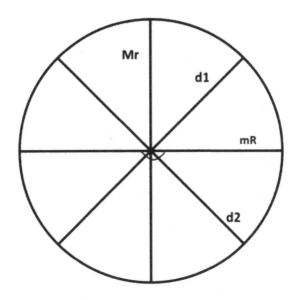

The major axis is considered as *Mr* and the minor axis is considered as *mR* and two diagonal points in an ellipse are denoted as *d1* and *d2*. The angle between *Mr* and *mR* is denoted as *a1* and the angle between *d1* and *d2* is denoted as *a2*. While *Mr* is not equal to *mR*, *d1=d2* and $\angle a1 = \angle a2 = 90°$, the object of interest is considered as a perfect ellipse (one) and for other values of *d1*, *d2*, *a1* and *a2*, the membership function value is below one. For a perfect ellipse, the value of $\mu_{EL}(x) = 1$ and the range of the membership value is [0, 1]. The logical representation of an ellipse is depicted in Figure 2 with the required parameters.

The membership function of the Square is presented below in Equation 3.

$$\mu_{SQ}(x) = e^{\left\{-\left[x_{sq}-1\right]^2\right\}} \tag{3}$$

This equation $\mu_{SQ}(x)$ is the membership function defined on squares *SQ*, and $x_{sq} = (Mr + d1) \big/ (mR + d2)$ is the parameter assigned to each square *(x)*. It is known that if $Mr = mR$ and $d1 = d2$, the shape of the object of interest is a perfect square and for other combination of values, the output value is less than one. The logical representation of square with Minimum and Maximum radius is depicted in Figure 3.

Figure 2. The logical representation of ellipse using minimum and maximum radius

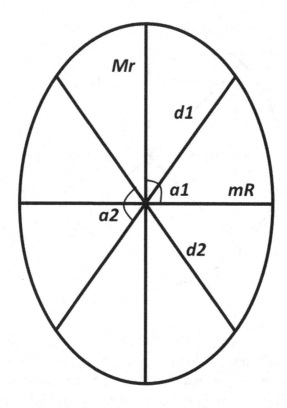

Figure 3. The logical representation of square using minimum and maximum radius

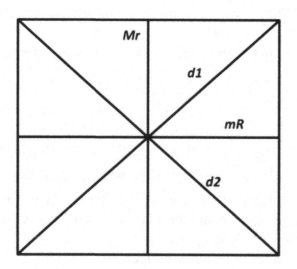

A four sided flat shape, where lines with all interior angles are right angles. The locations of the angles on the coordinate plane are determined by four vertices and opposite angles which are parallel and congruent. Also, the diagonal bisects each other and they are congruent. Considering Figure 1 and 3 for circle and square, both are perfect in their shape. In this case, the value of *Mr* and *mR* are the same for both the shapes. If there is a distortion in the shape, the values of *Mr* and *mR* change and their values are different. Thus, additional parameters are required to differentiate a perfect circle from a perfect square and as a result the *d1* and *d2* are introduced. For a perfect circle the value of *Mr=mR=d1=d2* and for square, *Mr=mR* and both *d1* and *d2* are different. Hence, *d1* and *d2* are used to distinguish between perfect circle and square. The logical representation of a rectangle with minimum and maximum radius is depicted in Figure 4. It is noticed from the figure that $mR \approx Mr$, $d1 \approx d2$ and angle *a1*, between *mR* and *Mr* is 900. However, a1 should not be equal to the angle between diagonals (*d1* and *d2*), i.e. $a1 \neq a2$. Using these variables, the fuzzy membership function for the rectangle is defined as below in Equation 4.

$$\mu_{REC}\left(x\right) = e^{\left\{-\left(x_{rec}-1\right)^2\right\}} \tag{4}$$

In this equation $\mu_{REC}\left(x\right)$ is the membership function defined on rectangles $REC\, x_{rec} = \left(\dfrac{d1-d2}{mR-Mr}\right)^2 + \left(\dfrac{\angle a1 + 90°}{\angle a2 + \left(180° - \angle a2\right)}\right)$ is the parameter assigned to each rectangle (x). It is observed from the equation that for $x_{rec}=1$, $\mu_{REC}\left(x\right) = 1$ and for $x_{rec} = 0.9$, the value of $\mu_{REC}\left(x\right) = 0.9$ and thus the fuzziness is captured.

A rhombus is a four sided shape with equal length on all sides. Also, opposite sides are parallel as well as opposite angles are equal. The diagonals *d1* and *d2* meet in the middle at right angles. The logical representation of a rhombus with minimum and maximum radius is shown in Figure 5. The fuzzy membership function using minimum and maximum radius for rhombus is given below in Equation 5 and it holds for *Mr* equal to *mR* and *d1* not equal to *d2*.

$$\mu_{RH}\left(x\right) = e^{\left\{-\left(x_{rh}-1\right)^2\right\}} \tag{5}$$

Figure 4. The logical representation of rectangle using minimum and maximum radius

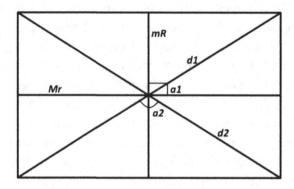

Figure 5. The logical representation of rhombus using minimum and maximum radius

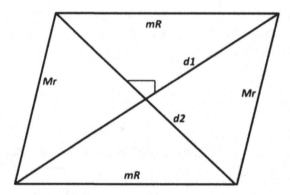

In the above equation, $\mu_{RH}(x)$ is the membership function defined over rhombuses *RH* and $x_{rh} = \left[mR * (d1 - d2) / Mr * (d1 - d2) \right]$ is the parameter assigned to each rhombus *(x)*, where $Mr = mR$ and $d1 \neq d2$.

A cone is a shape that has a circle at the bottom and sides that narrow to a point. The point at the end of a cone is called vertex. The logical representation of a cone is presented in Figure 6. The membership function of the cone is defined as follows.

$$\mu_{CN}(x) = e^{\left\{ -(x_{cn} - 1)^2 \right\}} \tag{6}$$

Figure 6. The logical representation of cone using minimum and maximum radius

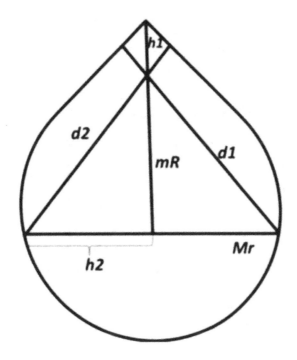

where $\mu_{CN}\left(x\right)$ is the membership function defined over cones *CN* and $x_{cn} = \left[\left(mR - Mr\right) * d1 \big/ \left(Mr - mR\right) * d2\right] + \left(h1 \big/ h2\right)$ is the parameter assigned to each cone *(x)*.

A solid object with two identical flat ends that are circular or elliptical and one curved side is called as Cylinder. The view of the cylinder is presented in Figure 7. The membership function for the cylinder is given in Equation 7.

$$\mu_{CY}\left(x\right) \ = \ e^{\left\{-\left(x_{cy}-1\right)^{2}\right\}} \tag{7}$$

Hence, $\mu_{CY}\left(x\right)$ is the membership function defined over cylinders *CY*, and $x_{cy} = \left[\left(mR - Mr\right) * d1 \big/ \left(Mr - mR\right) * d2\right] * \left(h1 \big/ h2\right)$ is the parameter assigned to each cylinder (x) where $mR \neq Mr$, $d1 = d2$ and $h1 = h2 \neq 0$.

Figure 7. The logical representation of cylinder using minimum and maximum radius

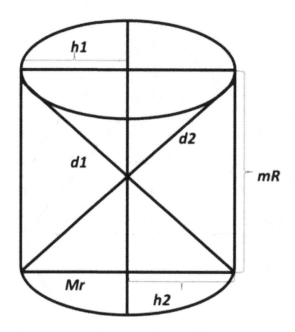

Computational Process of Fuzzy Membership Values

The computational process of the fuzzy membership values of the object is explained in this section.

Figure 8 portrays the mechanism of extracting an object and computation of the values of $r1, r2,...,rn$ $r1, r2,...,rn$ out of which minimum and maximum radius are chosen. Hence, the value Mr, mR, d_1 and d_2 are scaled to [0-1] range by normalizing their values. In Table 2, various combinations of values of the parameters of a circle are shown. Here, the value of Mr, mR, d_1 and d_2 vary from 0 to 1 and $\mu_C(x) = e^{\left\{-\left(x_c-1\right)^2\right\}}$ is calculated. For instance, Mr is varied from 0-1 in steps 0.1 and other values are fixed at 1. Similarly, in the next step, mR is varied between 0 and 1 in steps 0.1 and rests of the parameters are kept as constants. For all the combinations $\mu_C(x) = e^{\left\{-\left(x_c-1\right)^2\right\}}$ is calculated and the variation is presented in Figure 9.

Figure 9 depicts the variations among Mr, mR, $d1$ and $d2$. While Mr is varied slowly from 0 to 1, the membership value also varies with Mr from 0.8 to 1. Similarly, in Figure 9 *(b), (c)* and *(d)* the membership value is depicted

Figure 8. Illustration of object extraction and measuring radius (a) original image (b) object; silhouette (c) and (d) centroid computation using MATLAB Tool (e) computation of minimum and maximum radius and (f) MATLAB tool

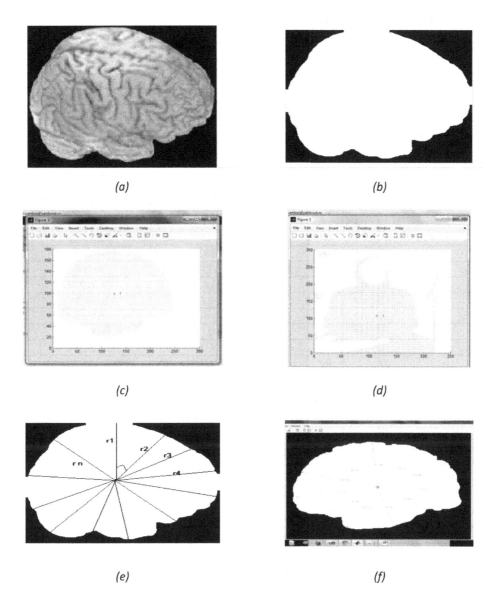

(a)

(b)

(c)

(d)

(e)

(f)

for mR, $d1$ and $d2$. It is noticed that mR shows smooth variation from 0.8 to 1, $d1$ shows smooth variation from 0.45 to 1 and $d2$ shows variation from 0.8 to 1. Thus, the parameter x_c captures the properties of radius and the diagonal

Table 2. The fuzzy membership values for different combination of parameters for circle

Mr	mR	d1	d2	(mr+Mr)/(d1+d2)	$\mu_C(x) = e^{\left\{-(x_c-1)^2\right\}}$
1	1	1	1	1	1
0.9	1	1	1	0.95	0.997503
0.8	1	1	1	0.9	0.99005
0.7	1	1	1	0.85	0.977751
0.6	1	1	1	0.8	0.960789
0.5	1	1	1	0.75	0.939413
0.4	1	1	1	0.7	0.913931
0.3	1	1	1	0.65	0.884706
0.2	1	1	1	0.6	0.852144
0.1	1	1	1	0.55	0.816686
1	0.9	1	1	0.95	0.997503
1	0.8	1	1	0.9	0.99005
1	0.7	1	1	0.85	0.977751
1	0.6	1	1	0.8	0.960789
1	0.5	1	1	0.75	0.939413
1	0.4	1	1	0.7	0.913931
1	0.3	1	1	0.65	0.884706
1	0.2	1	1	0.6	0.852144
1	0.1	1	1	0.55	0.816686
1	1	0.9	1	1.052631579	0.997234
1	1	0.8	1	1.111111111	0.98773
1	1	0.7	1	1.176470588	0.969338
1	1	0.6	1	1.25	0.939413
1	1	0.5	1	1.333333333	0.894839
1	1	0.4	1	1.428571429	0.832208
1	1	0.3	1	1.538461538	0.748308
1	1	0.2	1	1.666666667	0.64118
1	1	0.1	1	1.818181818	0.512005
1	1	1	0.9	1.052631579	0.997234
1	1	1	0.8	1.111111111	0.98773
1	1	1	0.7	1.176470588	0.969338
1	1	1	0.6	1.25	0.939413
1	1	1	0.5	1.333333333	0.894839
1	1	1	0.4	1.428571429	0.832208
1	1	1	0.3	1.538461538	0.748308
1	1	1	0.2	1.666666667	0.64118
1	1	1	0.1	1.818181818	0.512005

of a circle shape and calculates the fuzzy membership values with respect to the degree of deformation of the object.

Similarly, Table 3, the fuzzy membership values for different combination of parameters for an Ellipse are presented. In contrast to the content in Table 2, only the value for a minimum combination is provided. Here, *Mr* is varied from 0 to 1 in steps 0.1 by keeping other parameters constant and $\mu_{EL}(x) = e^{\{-x_{el}-1\}}$ is calculated. It is observed that the last column of the Table is the membership value and is smooth for capturing fuzzy boundary information of an ellipse. Similar to circle and ellipse, the values for other shapes can also be calculated.

RESULTS AND DISCUSSION OF FOSIR

The objects present in the images are extracted and for each object, the membership value is calculated to construct feature vector. The closeness of the object of interest with circle, ellipse, square, rectangle, rhombus, cone and cylinder is obtained. For all the database images, the membership values are calculated and stored in feature database. Given a query image, the feature is extracted and compared with the features in the feature database and ranked.

Figure 9. Sample values of different parameters for fuzzy membership functions defined over circles for various values of (a) Mr (b) mR (c) d1 (d) d2

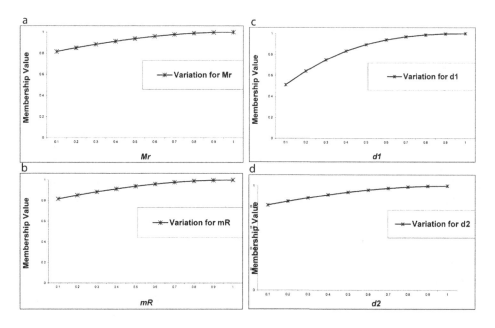

Table 3. The fuzzy membership values for different combination of parameters for an ellipse

Mr	mR	d1	d2	a1	a2	$\mu_{EL}\left(x\right)=e^{\left\{-x_{el}-1\right\}}$
0.9	1	0.9	1	0.9	0.1	0
0.8	1	0.8	1	0.8	0.2	1.13E-07
0.7	1	0.7	1	0.7	0.3	0.00432
0.6	1	0.6	1	0.6	0.4	0.105399
0.5	1	0.5	1	0.5	0.5	0.367879
0.4	1	0.4	1	0.4	0.6	0.64118
0.3	1	0.3	1	0.3	0.7	0.832208
0.2	1	0.2	1	0.2	0.8	0.939413
0.1	1	0.1	1	0.1	0.9	0.98773

The similarity between the query and database image is calculated using the similarity measure presented in Chapter 5. The performance of the proposed approach is evaluated using standard performance metrics such as Precision, Recall and Coefficient of Variation. As both the Precision and Recall are already defined, the Coefficient of Variation is given below.

$$\text{Coefficient of Variation} = \frac{\text{STD of Precision}}{\text{Mean Precision}} \qquad (8)$$

Li et al. (2014) and Li et al. (2015) have presented a comparative study on the performance of various shape based retrieval methods. However, the methods retrieved by the study is little older and as a result, the performance of FOSIR is compared with methods such as Li et al. (2009), Zagoris et al. (2011), Chahooki and Charkari (2012), Ayed et al. (2012), Frosini & Landi (2013), Tran et al. (2014), Hasegawa and Tabbone (2014), Deng et al. (2014) and Tanács et al. (2015) on various benchmark datasets. Initially, LabelMe benchmark dataset (http://cvcl.mit.edu/database.htm) with 9356 images is used in which 9144 object dominant images are categorized into 101 classes and 212 texture dominant images are categorized into 19 classes. Similar types of images are kept in the same folder structure and the classes are created based on certain semantic relevance among the images in a class, which is the ground truth. During retrieval, if an image in the retrieval set belongs to the query class, the image is relevant otherwise it is irrelevant. The retrieval is performed by a group of graduates and research students for calculating the Precision of retrieval for various Recall values. In fact, the Precision values are cross checked for 10% of the queries. The group has considered 2,500 object dominated images from various categories of LabelMe dataset as query images and the mean of Precision is calculated for all the 2,500 query images with ground-truth. The performance of FOSIR on LabelMe is presented in Table 4, where the Mean Precision of retrieval is shown for different Recall values. Results are obtained for different values of Recall from 0.1 to 1.0 in steps of 0.1 and the corresponding Precision is calculated. All the comparative methods have used the distance metric presented in Chapter 5. Higher the distance, the higher is the similarity between a query image and a target image. It is observed that FOSIR outperforms all the similar methods. It is noticed that the Precision of FOSIR holds during quite large values of Recall before they start to degrade. The performance by Chahooki and Charkari (2012) is low compared to all other methods. The performance by Li et al. (2009), Zagoris et al. (2011) and Frosini and Landi (2013) are quite similar and the performance of Deng et al. (2014) and Tanács et al. (2015) is closer to FOSIR and lower than FOSIR.

Besides having high value of mean Precision, it is also important for image retrieval systems to have a low standard deviation of Precision so that the quality of retrieval appears equally good for different observers. To study this, the standard deviation of Precision for all the methods is calculated and

Table 4. Recall vs. mean precision on LabelMe dataset

Approaches	Recall									
	0.1	0.2	0.3	0.4	0.5	0.6	0.7	0.8	0.9	1.0
FOSIR	0.98	0.96	0.93	0.90	0.88	0.86	0.86	0.84	0.81	0.75
Chahooki and Charkari	0.90	0.87	0.86	0.83	0.80	0.78	0.75	0.72	0.70	0.68
Ayed et al.	0.92	0.91	0.90	0.88	0.85	0.82	0.79	0.76	0.73	0.70
Li et al.	0.97	0.94	0.90	0.88	0.86	0.84	0.81	0.79	0.77	0.70
Zagoris et al.	0.97	0.95	0.91	0.89	0.87	0.85	0.83	0.80	0.78	0.70
Frosini and Landi	0.97	0.95	0.92	0.89	0.87	0.85	0.84	0.81	0.78	0.70
Tran et al.	0.97	0.95	0.92	0.895	0.871	0.852	0.843	0.82	0.785	0.712
Hasegawa and Tabbone	0.97	0.95	0.92	0.894	0.871	0.851	0.844	0.823	0.785	0.7132
Deng et al.	0.97	0.95	0.92	0.894	0.875	0.853	0.845	0.825	0.786	0.721
Tanács et al.	0.97	0.95	0.92	0.89	0.875	0.855	0.85	0.85	0.80	0.731

shown in Table 5. It is observed that the standard deviation with the FOSIR is low compared to other methods. The Standard Deviation of Chahooki and Charkari (2012) is very poor compared to all other methods. The performance of Zagoris et al. (2011), Frosini and Landi (2013) and Li et al (2009) is similar and the difference in the value of standard deviation of Precision between them is negligible. The performance of Tran et al. (2014), Hasegawa and Tabbone (2014) and Deng et al. (2014) have similar trend and Tanács et al. (2015) has little edge over these approaches. However, when compared to all, the performance of FOSIR is encouraging.

In addition to Mean and Standard Deviation of Precision, the Coefficient of Variation (CV) is calculated. It is defined as the ratio of the Standard Deviation to the Mean, which is the inverse of the definition of Signal-to-Noise ratio. It shows the extent of variability in relation to the Mean of the population. The Coefficient of Variation is computed only for data measured on a ratio scale, as these are measurements that can only take non-negative values. The Coefficient of Variation may not have any meaning for data on an interval scale. The Recall vs. Coefficient of Variation of Precision on a controlled database of 9356 images is presented in Table 6 and it is observed that the performance of FOSIR is good.

In addition to the results given above, the performance of FOSIR is evaluated on GRAZ-01 database developed by the Institute of Electrical Measurement and Measurement Signal Processing, Graz University of Technology (http://

Table 5. Recall vs. standard deviation of precision on LabelMe dataset

Approaches	Recall									
	0.1	0.2	0.3	0.4	0.5	0.6	0.7	0.8	0.9	1.0
FOSIR	**0.07**	**0.1**	**0.16**	**0.18**	**0.17**	**0.18**	**0.18**	**0.19**	**0.20**	**0.20**
Chahooki and Charkari	0.75	0.76	0.76	0.77	0.75	0.78	0.79	0.79	0.79	0.79
Ayed *et al.*	0.50	0.57	0.60	0.60	0.61	0.62	0.63	0.64	0.65	0.65
Li *et al.*	0.20	0.21	0.21	0.22	0.23	0.23	0.24	0.25	0.26	0.26
Zagoris *et al.*	0.18	0.20	0.21	0.21	0.22	0.22	0.23	0.25	0.25	0.25
Frosini and Landi	0.15	0.16	0.18	0.20	0.21	0.21	0.21	0.22	0.22	0.22
Tran *et al.*	0.11	0.12	0.11	0.20	0.20	0.21	0.21	0.21	0.21	0.216
Hasegawa and Tabbone	0.12	0.12	0.11	0.19	0.20	0.20	0.20	0.21	0.21	0.22
Deng *et al.*	0.11	0.13	0.13	0.19	0.19	0.20	0.21	0.22	0.22	0.22
Tanács *et al.*	0.10	0.12	0.12	0.19	0.18	0.19	0.20	0.20	0.20	0.209

Table 6. Recall vs. coefficient of variation of precision on LabelMe dataset

Approaches	Recall									
	0.1	0.2	0.3	0.4	0.5	0.6	0.7	0.8	0.9	1.0
FOSIR	**0.07**	**0.1**	**0.17**	**0.2**	**0.19**	**0.21**	**0.21**	**0.23**	**0.25**	**0.27**
Chahooki and Charkari	0.83	0.87	0.88	0.93	0.94	1.00	1.05	1.1	1.13	1.16
Ayed *et al*	0.54	0.63	0.67	0.68	0.72	0.76	0.8	0.84	0.89	0.93
Li *et al.*	0.21	0.22	0.23	0.25	0.27	0.27	0.3	0.32	0.34	0.37
Zagoris *et al.*	0.19	0.21	0.23	0.24	0.25	0.26	0.28	0.31	0.32	0.36
Frosini and Landi	0.15	0.17	0.19	0.22	0.24	0.24	0.25	0.27	0.28	0.31
Tran *et al.*	0.11	0.13	0.12	0.22	0.24	0.25	0.26	0.26	0.27	0.30
Hasegawa and Tabbone	0.12	0.13	0.12	0.21	0.24	0.24	0.25	0.26	0.28	0.31
Deng *et al.*	0.11	0.14	0.14	0.21	0.22	0.24	0.25	0.27	0.29	0.31
Tanács *et al.*	0.10	0.13	0.13	0.21	0.21	0.22	0.24	0.24	0.26	0.29

www.emt.tugraz.at/~pinz/data/GRAZ_01/) and Oxford Building Data Set (http://www.robots.ox.ac.uk/~vgg/data/oxbuildings/) developed by Visual Geometry Group, Department of Engineering Science, University of Oxford. The database consists of categories such as BIKES, PERSONS and BIKES and NO PERSONS, NO BIKES. In the bike category, four groups are maintained (image Nos. 001 to 373), four groups in person category (image Nos. 001-460), four groups in persons and bike (image Nos. 001 to 210) and finally two groups in No person and No bike category (image Nos. 001-273). The database consists of ground truth for the first 150 images belonging to bike category and it is being considered as ground truth in this work. In addition, the categories having images of different groups are numbered and considered as ground truth. During retrieval, for a query image belonging to a category (group), the retrieval set is verified. In the retrieval set, if an image belongs to the query group is found, it is considered as relevant, otherwise, it is taken as irrelevant. Similar to LabelMe data set, 10% of the retrieval set is verified manually by graduate and research students in our research group. The Oxford Buildings Dataset consists of 5062 images collected from Flickr (https://www.flickr.com/) by searching for particular Oxford landmarks. The collection has been manually annotated to generate a comprehensive ground truth for 11 different landmarks, each represented by 5 possible queries. The ground truth available with the data set is considered and in addition, the ground truth and 10% of the retrieval set is verified manually by students from our research group as it is done for other dataset.

Table 7. Recall vs. coefficient of variation of precision on GRAZ-01 dataset

Approaches	Recall									
	0.1	0.2	0.3	0.4	0.5	0.6	0.7	0.8	0.9	1.0
FOSIR	**0.06**	**0.08**	**0.09**	**0.12**	**0.14**	**0.17**	**0.18**	**0.21**	**0.23**	**0.24**
Chahooki and Charkari	0.76	0.8	0.83	0.87	0.92	0.95	0.98	1.03	1.06	1.1
Ayed *et al.*	0.6	0.63	0.69	0.72	0.74	0.76	0.81	0.84	0.86	0.93
Li *et al.*	0.27	0.29	0.31	0.34	0.36	0.37	0.39	0.41	0.43	0.47
Zagoris *et al.*	0.22	0.24	0.26	0.28	0.31	0.32	0.34	0.35	0.38	0.41
Frosini and Landi	0.19	0.19	0.19	0.21	0.22	0.25	0.27	0.3	0.31	0.33
Tran *et al.*	0.11	0.12	0.11	0.18	0.20	0.23	0.24	0.26	0.28	0.31
Hasegawa and Tabbone	0.10	0.11	0.11	0.17	0.20	0.23	0.23	0.25	0.28	0.29
Deng *et al.*	0.10	0.11	0.13	0.18	0.19	0.22	0.22	0.25	0.27	0.29
Tanács *et al.*	0.09	0.10	0.10	0.16	0.18	0.21	0.22	0.24	0.25	0.26

In addition to all the results presented above, other benchmark datasets are also considered, where the content of the images is natural scenery and the background and foreground have similar color property. The object content of the images is also very less. Below in Table 9, performance evaluation of the FOSIR is given on MIT saliency benchmark dataset (http://saliency. mit.edu/downloads.html). This database consists of 300 natural images and has been developed for the eye tracking problem. The relevant set is manually found using the same student group and the performance for 50

Table 8. Recall vs. coefficient of variation of precision on Oxford Building dataset

Approaches	Recall									
	0.1	0.2	0.3	0.4	0.5	0.6	0.7	0.8	0.9	1.0
FOSIR	**0.05**	**0.09**	**0.13**	**0.16**	**0.2**	**0.22**	**0.25**	**0.26**	**0.29**	**0.31**
Chahooki and Charkari	0.95	0.97	1	1.03	1.09	1.12	1.16	1.2	1.23	1.29
Ayed *et al.*	0.73	0.75	0.77	0.8	0.84	0.88	0.9	0.92	0.96	1
Li *et al.*	0.34	0.37	0.39	0.4	0.42	0.44	0.48	0.51	0.54	0.56
Zagoris *et al.*	0.32	0.35	0.36	0.39	0.42	0.44	0.45	0.48	0.49	0.52
Frosini and Landi	0.23	0.24	0.25	0.29	0.31	0.32	0.33	0.35	0.36	0.39
Tran *et al.*	0.11	0.12	0.19	0.22	0.23	0.28	0.33	0.35	0.36	0.39
Hasegawa and Tabbone	0.13	0.13	0.19	0.23	0.27	0.30	0.33	0.35	0.36	0.39
Deng *et al.*	0.20	0.22	0.23	0.26	0.26	0.29	0.33	0.35	0.36	0.39
Tanács *et al.*	0.09	0.10	0.18	0.21	0.23	0.26	0.29	0.33	0.34	0.34

Table 9. Recall vs. mean precision on MIT Saliency dataset

Approaches	Recall									
	0.1	0.2	0.3	0.4	0.5	0.6	0.7	0.8	0.9	1.0
FOSIR	**0.85**	**0.84**	**0.82**	**0.80**	**0.77**	**0.76**	**0.74**	**0.71**	**0.68**	**0.65**
Chahooki and Charkari	0.78	0.75	0.72	0.69	0.67	0.65	0.62	0.60	0.58	0.55
Ayed *et al.*	0.78	0.77	0.75	0.74	0.73	0.70	0.68	0.67	0.65	0.63
Li *et al.*	0.65	0.63	0.61	0.59	0.58	0.56	0.54	0.52	0.51	0.50
Zagoris *et al.*	0.75	0.73	0.70	0.68	0.66	0.63	0.61	0.59	0.58	0.57
Frosini and Landi	0.80	0.78	0.76	0.74	0.71	0.70	0.68	0.66	0.64	0.62
Tran *et al.*	0.81	0.78	0.77	0.75	0.70	0.73	0.70	0.67	0.64	0.62
Hasegawa and Tabbone	0.81	0.78	0.77	0.76	0.71	0.73	0.71	0.66	0.63	0.62
Deng *et al.*	0.82	0.80	0.79	0.77	0.71	0.73	0.71	0.67	0.65	0.62
Tanács *et al.*	0.83	0.81	0.80	0.78	0.75	0.73	0.72	0.68	0.65	0.62

queries. In contrast to all the results given above, the performance of FOSIR is not encouraging. This is due to the fact that the images of natural scenery are not object dominant and as a result, poses difficulties while separating different objects present in the images. However, the performance of FOSIR is convincing compared to other similar approaches.

Also, the image collection of the IAPR TC-12 Benchmark dataset (http://imageclef.org/photodata) with 20,000 still natural images are taken from locations around the world that comprise of an assorted cross-section of still natural images. This includes pictures of different sports and actions, photographs of people, animals, cities, landscapes and many other aspects of contemporary life. Each image is associated with a text caption in English, German and Spanish. These annotations are stored in a database, which is managed by a benchmark administration system that allows the specification of parameters according to which different subsets of the image collection can be generated. The ground truth in our work is generated by the group of students based on the annotations available in the dataset and the Precision Vs. Recall is calculated for 100 query images from different categories. It is observed from the Table 10 that FOSIR holds the Precision till the end and the Precision value is also high when compared to others.

Below, the image database from the University of Washington (http://imagedatabase.cs.washington.edu/groundtruth/) is used for evaluating the performance. There are 23 classes, stored in a directory structure with a directory name as the image category name. For measuring the ground

Table 10. Recall vs. mean precision on IAPR TC-12 dataset

Approaches	Recall									
	0.1	0.2	0.3	0.4	0.5	0.6	0.7	0.8	0.9	1.0
FOSIR	**0.91**	**0.89**	**0.87**	**0.85**	**0.84**	**0.82**	**0.80**	**0.79**	**0.77**	**0.74**
Chahooki and Charkari	0.88	0.85	0.83	0.81	0.79	0.77	0.75	0.71	0.68	0.65
Ayed *et al.*	0.87	0.85	0.84	0.82	0.80	0.78	0.75	0.74	0.72	0.69
Li *et al.*	0.85	0.84	0.82	0.80	0.78	0.77	0.74	0.70	0.67	0.64
Zagoris *et al.*	0.86	0.84	0.82	0.79	0.76	0.74	0.72	0.69	0.66	0.64
Frosini and Landi	0.88	0.86	0.84	0.82	0.80	0.77	0.74	0.73	0.70	0.68
Tran *et al.*	0.88	0.87	0.85	0.83	0.81	0.78	0.74	0.72	0.70	0.68
Hasegawa and Tabbone	0.88	0.87	0.84	0.82	0.82	0.79	0.76	0.74	0.72	0.70
Deng *et al.*	0.88	0.87	0.84	0.83	0.81	0.80	0.77	0.75	0.73	0.71
Tanács *et al.*	0.89	0.88	0.85	0.83	0.82	0.80	0.77	0.76	0.76	0.72

truth, the directory name is being used by the student group using which the evaluation is performed. The result is shown in Table 11.

Based on the results presented in Table 4 – 11, using various controlled databases, it is noticed that the Fuzzy-Object-Shape outperforms all the other similar approaches. This is due to the fact that most of the images contain object level information, which can be used as feature for discriminating one from another. The Fuzzy-Object-Shape based representation scheme effectively captures the object information using a suitable fuzzy membership function

Table 11. Recall vs. mean precision on UW dataset

Approaches	Recall									
	0.1	0.2	0.3	0.4	0.5	0.6	0.7	0.8	0.9	1.0
FOSIR	**0.82**	**0.80**	**0.78**	**0.75**	**0.74**	**0.73**	**0.72**	**0.71**	**0.70**	**0.69**
Chahooki and Charkari	0.78	0.77	0.75	0.73	0.71	0.68	0.65	0.63	0.62	0.60
Ayed *et al.*	0.76	0.75	0.73	0.72	0.70	0.68	0.65	0.64	0.62	0.60
Li *et al.*	0.70	0.69	0.68	0.65	0.63	0.61	0.60	0.59	0.58	0.56
Zagoris *et al.*	0.77	0.76	0.75	0.73	0.71	0.70	0.68	0.67	0.66	0.64
Frosini and Landi	0.80	0.79	0.78	0.76	0.73	0.71	0.70	0.68	0.66	0.64
Tran *et al.*	0.80	0.78	0.77	0.75	0.73	0.72	0.70	0.69	0.65	0.64
Hasegawa and Tabbone	0.79	0.77	0.76	0.74	0.72	0.70	0.69	0.68	0.66	0.67
Deng *et al.*	0.80	0.79	0.77	0.76	0.75	0.71	0.70	0.69	0.67	0.66
Tanács *et al.*	0.80	0.79	0.77	0.73	0.72	0.71	0.70	0.69	0.68	0.67

with minimum and maximum radii values. The extracted values effectively discriminated the query object with the database object. Also, the similarity measure presented in Chapter 5 complements the feature vector and removes the averaging effect by Integrated Region Matching (IRM). Further, while observing the result presented in Table 4 – 11, FOSIR achieves lower Precision for various Recall. This is due to the fact that these image datasets contain images without clear boundaries. All these images are natural scenery and thus, objects overlap with each other, which influence the result.

In addition to all the above results on controlled database, it is also important to evaluate the performance of FOSIR in an uncontrolled image data set. The FOSIR have used crawled 40,000 images from the Internet and created a feature database. Since there is no possibility to measure the ground truth, only Precision is used as evaluation parameter and the same student group has performed the query and thus the Precision is calculated. The relevant image in the retrieval set is identified by the user who is performing the search and the same team is used for calculating the Precision for 1000 queries. The Precision is calculated for the NN 2, 5, 10, 15 and 20 and presented below in Table 12.

It is observed that the Precision value of Chahooki and Charkari (2012), Ayed et al. (2012), Li et al. (2009), Zagoris et al. (2011) and Frosini and Landi (2013) is in similar range and the Precision of Frosini and Landi (2013) is higher than all of these methods. Tran et al. (2014), Hasegawa and Tabbone (2014), Deng et al. (2014) and Tanács et al. (2015) are maintaining a range and however, the performance of FOSIR is encouraging when compared with all these methods and thus, Precision is higher than all the comparative methods.

CONCLUSION

The content of the images such as color, texture and shape can be used for effectively discriminating the images. Compared to color and texture, the shape is considered as an important feature for many real-time applications, say CBIR. In this chapter, Fuzzy-Object-Shape is presented for extracting the shape information present in the images. Images are segmented into non-overlapping clusters and are treated as objects. The geometric properties of these objects are extracted using minimum and maximum radius of the objects. It is further noticed that the boundary of the object is ill-defined and there is impreciseness and vagueness in the object information. The closeness of each object with well-known primitive shapes are estimated. It is known that the

Table 12. Precision on uncontrolled database of 40,000 images

Approaches	Nearest Neighbour				
	P @2	P @5	P@10	P@15	P@20
FOSIR	**0.975**	**0.96**	**0.95**	**0.94**	**0.93**
Chahooki and Charkari	0.85	0.84	0.82	0.81	0.79
Ayed *et al.*	0.82	0.80	0.79	0.78	0.77
Li *et al.*	0.89	0.87	0.86	0.84	0.82
Zagoris *et al.*	0.88	0.87	0.85	0.83	0.82
Frosini and Landi	0.91	0.89	0.87	0.86	0.85
Tran *et al.*	0.90	0.89	0.87	0.85	0.84
Hasegawa and Tabbone	0.91	0.89	0.87	0.85	0.83
Deng *et al.*	0.92	0.90	0.88	0.86	0.84
Tanács *et al.*	0.93	0.91	0.89	0.88	0.86

impreciseness can be effectively captured by fuzzy functions and FOS has proposed seven fuzzy membership function for the same. The value of each fuzzy membership function are constructed as feature vector to define the properties of individual objects. A large number of well-known bench mark datasets are used for rigorous performance evaluation of FOS. For each data set, Precision, Recall and Co-Efficient of Variance is presented, analyzed and discussed. The performance is compared with similar approaches and found that FOS is good in retrieving relevant images.

REFERENCES

Abbasi, S., Mokhtarian, F., & Kittler, J. (1999). Curvature Scale Space Image in Shape Similarity Retrieval. Multimedia Systems, (7), 467–476.

Alhabashneh, , Iqbal, Doctor, & James. (2017). Fuzzy rule based profiling approach for enterprise information seeking and retrieval. *Information Sciences, 394–395*, 18–37.

Ayed, B., Kardouchi, S., & Selouani, S. A. (2012). Rotation invariant Fuzzy Shape Contexts based on Eigen shapes and Fourier transforms for efficient Radiological image retrieval. *Proceedings of International Conference on Multimedia Computing and Systems (ICMCS)*, 26 –271.

Belongie, S., Malik, J., & Puzicha, J. (2002). Shape Matching and Object Recognition using Shape Contexts. *IEEE Transactions on Pattern Analysis and Machine Intelligence*, *24*(4), 509–522. doi:10.1109/34.993558

Chahooki, M. A. Z., & Charkari, N. M. (2012). Supervised Shape Retrieval based on Fusion of Multiple Feature Spaces. *Proceedings of 20th Iranian Conference on Electrical Engineering (ICEE'12)*, 1072-1074. doi:10.1109/IranianCEE.2012.6292512

Colombo, C., Bimbo, A. D., & Pala, P. (1999). Semantics in Visual Information Retrieval. *IEEE MultiMedia*, *6*(3), 38–53. doi:10.1109/93.790610

Deng, Z., Xiao, K., & Huang, J. (2014). A New Fuzzy Shape Context Approach Based on Multi-clue and State Reservoir Computing. *Proceedings of International Joint Conference on Neural Networks (IJCNN'14)*, 2361-2366. doi:10.1109/IJCNN.2014.6889800

El-Ghazal, Basir, & Belkasim. (2007). A new shape signature for Fourier descriptors. *Proceedings of 14th IEEE International Conference on Image Processing (ICIP'07)*, 161-164.

Flickner, M., Sawhney, H., Niblack, W., Ashley, J., Huang, Q., Dom, B., & Yanker, P. et al. (1995). Query By Image and Video Content: The QBIC System. *Computer Magazine*, *28*(9), 23–32. doi:10.1109/2.410146

Frosini, P., & Landi, C. (2013). Persistent Betti numbers for a noise tolerant shape based approach to image retrieval. *Pattern Recognition Letters*, *34*(8), 863–872. doi:10.1016/j.patrec.2012.10.015

Hasegawa, M., & Tabbone, S. (2014). Amplitude-only log Radon transform for geometric invariant shape descriptor. *Pattern Recognition*, *47*(2), 643–658. doi:10.1016/j.patcog.2013.07.024

Islam, Banerjee, Bhattacharyya, & Chakraborty. (2017). Content-based image retrieval based on multiple extended fuzzy-rough framework. *Applied Soft Computing*, *57*, 102–117.

Latecki, L., & Lakamper, R. (2000). Shape similarity measure based on correspondence of visual parts. *IEEE Transactions on Pattern Analysis and Machine Intelligence*, *22*(10), 1185–1190. doi:10.1109/34.879802

Li, Lu, Gidil, Schreck, Bustos, Ferreira, … Saavedra. (2014). A Comparison of methods for Sketch-based 3D shape retrieval. Computer Vision and Image Understanding, 119, 57-80.

Li, Lu, Li, Godil, Schreck, Aono, … Zou. (2015). A Comparison of 3D shape retrieval methods based on a large-scale benchmanrk supporting multimodal queries. Computer Vision and Image Understanding, 131, 1-27.

Li, Q., Luo, S., & Shi, Z. (2009). Fuzzy aesthetic semantics description and extraction for art image retrieval. *Computers and Mathematics with Applications, 57*(6), 1000–1009. doi:10.1016/j.camwa.2008.10.058

Mokhtarian, F., & Mackworth, A. (1992). A Theory of multiscale, curvature-based shape representation for planar curves. *IEEE Transactions on Pattern Analysis and Machine Intelligence, 14*(8), 789–805. doi:10.1109/34.149591

Tanács, A., Lindblad, J., Sladoje, N., & Kato, Z. (2015). Estimation of linear deformations of 2D and 3D fuzzy objects. *Pattern Recognition, 48*(4), 1391–1403. doi:10.1016/j.patcog.2014.10.006

Tran, T. T., Pham, V. T., & Shyu, K. K. (2014). Image segmentation using fuzzy energy-based active contour with shape prior. *Journal of Visual Communication Image Representation, 25*(7), 1732–1745. doi:10.1016/j.jvcir.2014.06.006

Zagoris, K., Ergina, K., & Papamarkos, N. (2011). Image retrieval systems based on compact shape descriptor and relevance feedback information. *Journal of Visual Communication and Image Representation, 22*(5), 378–390. doi:10.1016/j.jvcir.2011.03.002

Chapter 4
Encoding and Indexing Fuzzy Object Shape for Image Retrieval

ABSTRACT

The recent retrieval and indexing approaches suffer from the issues of curse of dimensionality, overlapping of vectors, need of extra parameters for clustering and not supporting incremental indexing. In this chapter, an indexing approach is introduced without enduring the above specified issues. The suggested indexing structure is dynamically rearranged based on the occurrences of pattern for merging the common patterns in low-level feature. Further, the feature is encoded using GR coding scheme and the feature database space required is reduced considerably. While there are many encoding scheme available, in this chapter GR coding is used for simplicity and its applicability. In addition, the compression ratio is discussed and numerical statistics is depicted. Overall, indexing scheme reduces the search space by following predetermined pattern for clustering. The encoding scheme reduces the size of the feature database and also achieves good precision of retrieval.

INTRODUCTION

Indexing is very important for image retrieval applications. It is imperative that a suitable indexing mechanism is required for effectively indexing low-level feature. The indexed feature can be combined with textual feature for

DOI: 10.4018/978-1-5225-3796-0.ch004

facilitating shape based retrieval. Broadly, there are two categories of indexing schemes namely vector quantization and multidimensional indexing. The multidimensional indexing is further divided into space-partitioning and data-partitioning methods. These methods represent the data in a hierarchical tree by splitting the data space progressively into smaller parts. The difference between these approaches is the way the data or space is divided. In space-partitioning, the *KD-tree* (K-Dimensional tree) splits the feature space into predefined hyper-planes, irrespective of the feature vector distribution. Such areas are disjoint and their combination covers the whole space. The main problem of *KD-tree* is that it is difficult to recognize the position of the feature vector using each level of the tree. Further, fixed partitioning of space can result to an empty or few populated cluster particularly in high dimensions. The R-tree, SS-tree and Sphere/Rectangle-tree are the most popular data partitioning approaches. The database items are distributed to partition the feature space. The R-tree represents each node in the tree as hyper-rectangle by partitioning the space. The space is again partitioned into smaller for representing the child nodes. The performance of *R-tree* is encouraging compared to *KD-tree* and it is found that the bounding rectangles are overlapping. It has outperformed *SS-tree*, where the minimum bounding spheres are used. However, the overlapping of higher dimensions is not fully rectified in the *SS–tree* also. The *SR-tree* is an enhancement of the *R-tree* and *SS-tree*, where the intersection of hyper-spheres and hyper-rectangles are performed to decide the shape of a partition. Due to the curse of dimensionality, the multidimensional indexing does not scale up well to high dimensional spaces.

In addition, the partitions increase exponentially with the dimension. However, these multidimensional indexing structures are mostly useful for medium dimensional feature spaces. The Principal Component Analysis (*PCA*) and Latent Semantic Indexing (*LSI*) have avoided the curse of dimensionality problem and reduced the dimension of feature vectors considerably for retrieval applications. The original feature vectors are considered as approximate of low dimensional transformed feature vectors. However, the most serious problem with these methods is that there is a loss of significant information due to reduction in the dimension of the feature vector. The distance computation is another multidimensional indexing based approach and it is observed that this approach is costly and CPU intensive, especially for high dimensional data spaces. Moreover, while a query point is located near a partition border of a nearest neighbor query algorithm, the performance degrades. This is due to the fact that it is necessary to take two decisions. For decreasing the retrieval time, the neighboring partitions are avoided or otherwise consider the neighboring partitions with high computational requirements.

Indexing Fuzzy-Object-Shape Feature

Though, the color and texture are prominent in visual appearance, shape is considered as one of the important low-level features in various image retrieval systems. This is due to the fact that the shape features can capture the most relevant and visual information, which is based on human perception (Ardizzoni, Bartolini & Patella, 1999). Human perceive scenes of the images as a composition of individual objects and is suitably identified by their shapes. Once the images are visualized in terms of individual objects, they can be effectively used for image retrieval applications. For retrieval, the similarity between the database and query images is calculated using K-Nearest Neighbor (*K-NN*) search. It is a linear search and requires $O(n)$ distance computation where n is the number of low-level features (vectors) in the database and it is too expensive for large value of n. An indexing scheme especially for shape retrieval is required to improve the retrieval time considerably by presenting the retrieval set very fast to the user.

The vector quantization approaches are alternative to the multidimensional techniques for generating image indexing scheme. Existing algorithms related to quantization schemas are mean shift based clustering (Jurie & Triggs, 2005), hierarchical K-means (Nister & Stewenius, 2006), agglomerative clustering (Leibe, Mikolajczyk & Schiele, 2006), randomized trees (Moosmann, Triggs & Jurie, 2008) and Self Organizing Maps (SOM) (Kaski, Kangas & Kohonen, 1998). In these algorithms, a set of data item is allocated into certain group so that the data items in the same group are considered more related to other groups and those groups are signified by its centroid or single representative data item. It is enough to validate the query point with centroid rather than validating with entire data items. The similarity measure is used to select the best group (or) groups and the data items exist in those groups are calculated to return the *K-NN*. While the dimensionality of the input vector is high, these algorithms endure from the expensive distance computation. Prior to clustering, the majority of these algorithms need to know the knowledge about the number of clusters, the initial partitions and the learning weights. However, it is noticed that these aspects are uncommon in the case of indexing framework. Besides SOM algorithm, many of these algorithms do not maintain the topological ordering of the data space. Recently, Qian & Tagare (2010) proposed an indexing algorithm using tree structure. The greedy and optimal tree adaptation procedures are derived for improving the indexing efficiency. This approach has considered the average number of node test incurred during the retrieval. The performance of the tree is mathematically encouraging. However, it suffers from space overlapping problem (Mejdoub, Fonteles, BenAmar & Antonini, 2009). The indexing approaches (Rusinol, Borras & Llados, 2010) and (Liu & Yap, 2012) are domain-specific in nature and it is difficult to extend them for a generic application problem Poursistami *et al*, (2013) have proposed vector quantization technique by extracting features from JPEG compressed images. A partial decoding procedure is applied and the indexing procedure is followed. A suitable codebook was generated using K-means algorithm to construct Discrete Cosine Transformation histogram. However, the time taken for partial decoding and the size of the code book is on the higher side. The query is indexed by exploiting certain properties of the query object itself (Barrios, Bustos & Skopal, 2014) is contrast to the most of the existing research. The query is processed online and thus the preprocessing step can be eliminated. This indexing scheme is suitable only for a sequence of query objects say video frames, with small distance between the consecutive query objects and may not be suitable for single image query system.

All these shape based features describe the shape properties and thus ignores the impreciseness and vagueness present in the shape of the object. The impreciseness may be captured by using fuzzy logic approach (Colombo, Bimbo & Pala, 1999) and have advocated a syntactic construction of a compositional semantics to build the semantic representation of images. A Linguistic Expression Based Image Description (LEBID), which is a fuzzy semantics description framework has been proposed to validate its feasibility in texture image retrieval (Li, Luo & Shi, 2009). It is noticed that prior knowledge is required to describe the image and fuzzy rules.

The feature-weighted Receptive Field (fwRF) is an encoding model designed to balance expressiveness, interpretability and scalability. The fwRF is organized around the notion of a feature map—a transformation of visual stimuli into visual features that preserves the topology of visual space. The key assumption of the fwRF model is that activity in each voxel encodes variation in a spatially localized region across multiple feature maps. This region is fixed for all feature maps; however, the contribution of each feature map to voxel activity is weighted (St-Yves & Naselaris 2017) and auto encoder is proposed for training using particle swam optimization (Sui., Bennamoun & Togneri 2017).

In this chapter, an indexing scheme is presented to form a cluster using dominant shape properties. The preprocessing technique reduces the space of feature database. Also, the shape feature, which is represented as histogram is encoded to reduce the size of the feature database. The textual information is used effectively and also combined with shape information for improving the performance of the retrieval. The performance of the approach is evaluated with well-known search engine system and it is found that the precision of retrieval is good.

INDEXING FUZZY OBJECT SHAPE FEATURE

The Fuzzy-Object-Shape (FOS) is represented as a feature vector, which is constructed as histogram having seven as its minimum dimension in which each index represents a primitive shape details. Given a large number of images, the FOS feature (histogram) is extracted and stored in the feature database. During retrieval, each feature vector in the database is accessed, compared, similarity is calculated and ranked. This approach increases the retrieval time and size of the feature database. Hence, a suitable indexing mechanism is required to index the FOS features for reducing the retrieval time. The FOS feature is indexed based on shape patterns and the dominant shape is identified from the feature values. The feature is encoded using Golombo-Rice (GR) (Golombo, 1966) encoding method so that the size of the feature database is reduced.

Consider FOSV as a set of FOS feature vector and is represented as below:

$$FOSV = \left\{ fosv_1, fosv_2, \dots fosv_n \right\} \tag{1}$$

Here, n represents the size of the feature database and each fos_i represents the feature of an image, which is a set of points in k-dimensional space. Initially, each feature of feature database is analyzed to identify the dominant shape property. Say for example, fos_i may have a value to indicate that it is a circle and ellipse dominant. Similarly, other fos_j may have dominant values for square, cone, etc. Thus, the dominant information of each fos_i is used for establishing an unique pattern and the fos_i having similar patterns are combined (vector quantization approach) into a group, which is uniquely identified by the pattern for indexing. The *Equation* 1 shows the feature database and the content of each feature vector, fos_i is shown in *Equation* 2.

$$fos_i = \left\{ circle_i, square_i, ellipse_i, rect_i, rho_i, cone_i, cylinder_i \right\} \qquad (2)$$

It is noticed from *Equation* 2 that each index has a numeric value using which the dominant points are calculated. For instance, given a fos_i with dominant value as circle and rectangle, the pattern of fos_i is established as *C-R* and rest of the index values are ignored. As a result, fos_i is represented as follows.

$$fos_i = \left\{ C - R \right\} \qquad (3)$$

In the above *Equation* 3, *C* and *R* represents circle and rectangle respectively. By applying the above logic, the initial clusters are defined as follows.

$$C^{FOSV} = \left\{ c_1, c_2, \ldots c_m \right\} \qquad (4)$$

The pattern of each cluster in *Equation* 4 is given below as

$$P_C^{FOSV} = \left\{ p_1, p_2, \ldots p_m \right\} \qquad (5)$$

In *Equation* 4, each cluster (c_i) contains many vectors and each of them may/may not have similar patterns. Based on a predefined quantization level, the similar features are grouped together. For instance, while the number of items in a cluster is very small, it may not adequately define the uniqueness of a pattern and has very little difference with the neighboring cluster. Thus, it is essential to combine a cluster with neighboring cluster, which is done iteratively till each cluster finally contains sufficient number of feature vector. This is achieved by defining a threshold on the number of feature vector in a cluster.

The threshold value is *c* and assumes that the clusters *c1*, *c2* and *c3* have 12, 7 and 7 numbers of features with patterns *p1*, *p2* and *p3*. If *p1=C-R-E*, *P2 = E-R-Co* and *P3 = E-R-Cy*, *c2* and *c3* are combined together by creating new cluster *c4* with patterns *p4= E-R* having 12 vectors (*c=12*). Here, the *Co* and *Cy* of *p2* and *p3* are discarded and the new cluster is formed with *p4=E-R*. This procedure is continued till each cluster contains sufficient number of feature vectors and stops when the dimension of the features in the cluster is at least one. The final clusters are formed with their patterns and the sample feature space is presented in Table 1. For simplicity, only five vectors are considered and presented for discussion. It is noticed that some of the index values are zero.and may not have any significance in representing the corresponding shape. The index having significant value alone is considered and the one with zero is discarded and is shown in Table 2. The dominant values are replaced with corresponding symbols and are depicted in Table 2 as *C* stands for Circle; *S* stands for Square and so on.

In Table 3, the truncated dominant feature values with their corresponding symbol is presented. It is known that the numeric value in various bins of low-level feature extracted from images is very low and sometimes zero. This approach effectively removes the space occupied by them and the feature is represented in compact as depicted in Table 3.

In Table 4, the relationship between the patterns and features is presented. The *C-S-E-R* pattern is considered as a pattern, which points out feature fos_1 and similarly all other patterns are selected to other feature vectors. In Table 5, the relationship between the patterns and combined feature is presented. While *C-S-R-Rh* and *C-S-R-Co* are combined together with k-dominant point 3, *C-S-R* is created as new pattern and is used as indexing for fos_4 and fos_5. Similarly, when new features are added to the feature repository, the pattern is generated and combined with the other neighboring pattern based on *K*-dominant point threshold value.

Table 1. Sample feature value

FOSV	Circle	Square	Ellipse	Rectangle	Rhombus	Cone	Cylinder
fos_1	0.65	0.32	0.43	0.76	0.00	0.000	0.000
fos_2	0.00	0.00	0.00	0.76	0.65	0.32	0.43
fos_3	0.00	0.00	0.67	0.432	0.65	0.000	0.000
fos_4	0.76	0.98	0.00	0.654	0.86	0.000	0.000
fos_5	0.76	0.98	0.00	0.654	0.00	0.860	0.000

Table 2. Dominant feature values with their symbols

FOSV	Circle	Square	Ellipse	Rectangle	Rhombus	Cone	Cylinder
fos_1	C	S	E	R			
fos_2				R	Rh	Co	Cy
fos_3			E	R	Rh		
fos_4	C	S		R	Rh		
fos_5	C	S		R		Co	

Table 3. Truncated dominant feature values with their symbols

FOSV	Pattern			
fos_1	C	S	E	R
fos_2	R	Rh	Co	Cy
fos_3	E	R	Rh	
fos_4	C	S	R	Rh
fos_5	C	S	R	Co

The FOS feature is combined with the textual feature for improving the Precision of retrieval and facilitates query refinement mechanism. Since, the keyword is not available along with most of the image database, large number of images are crawled from WWW for implementing query refinement. In Figure 1 (a), the architecture of feature extraction procedure is depicted. The crawler tool fetches the HTML documents along with the images from WWW. The images and text part of the document are separated by the document processing unit. The text part contains HTML TAGs along with the text information and the images are stored in a separate repository. The HTML TAG is parsed and stop words are removed from the documents for

Table 4. Relationship between the patterns and features

Patterns	FOSV
C-S-E-R	fos_1
R-Rh-Co-Cy	fos_2
E-R-Rh	fos_3
C-S-R-Rh	fos_4
C-S-R-Co	fos_5

Table 5. Relationship between the patterns and combined features

Patterns	FOSV
C-S-E-R	fos_1
R-Rh-Co-Cy	fos_2
E-R-Rh	fos_3
C-S-R	fos_4 fos_5

easy processing. A shape-TERM DB repository is created, which consists of shape related terms along with synonyms, hyponyms and hypernyms. For each term in the document, the synonyms, hyponyms and hypernyms are also found and compared with the terms in shape-TERM DB for creating pattern and document DB. On the other hand, for images, the FOS feature is extracted and FOS DB is created.

The retrieval scheme is shown in Figure 1 *(b)*, which contains scheme for both image and text based query. The query is presented in the form of text and the pattern of the text is identified along with the relationship between the text and document. All the images appeared in those documents are matched and their feature alone is extracted from FOS feature database. The final retrieval set is presented with matching the pattern of the query keyword and

Figure 1. Feature Extraction and Retrieval Scheme. (a) FOS Feature Extraction from WWW for Constructing Feature and TERM Databases (b) Retrieval procedure

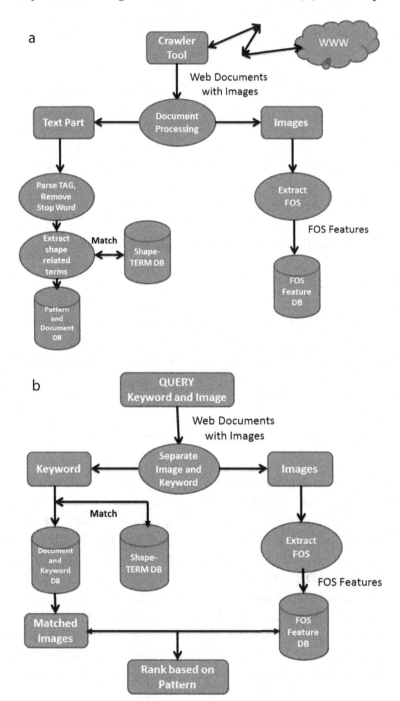

the images in the corresponding pattern of the cluster. In contrast, when image alone is presented as query, the first K-dominant points in the query image are identified and hence, the pattern is extracted. The cluster is identified in the feature database and only the similarity between the features in the cluster is calculated. Finally, the retrieval set is given to the user by ranking based on the distance value. The vector with the lowest distance is ranked top and the higher are ranked at the bottom. This indexing approach handles the vector overlap issue and the quality of the cluster is preserved. Further, no additional information is required for preserving the topological ordering of vectors. This is very much useful for multimedia databases, which grows with the time.

ENCODING FUZZY OBJECT SHAPE FEATURE

The scheme for encoding contains three stages such as indexing, encoding and similarity measure. The schematic diagram is depicted in Figure 2. In the primary stage, an indexing scheme is suggested, where the dimension of the shape feature, represented as histogram is used for indexing and in the second stage, the indexed histograms are encoded using Golombo-Rice coding method (Golombo, 1966). In the third stage, a new distance measure named Common Bins Similarity Measure (CBSM) is presented, where the common bin indices between the query and database histograms are used to calculate the distance. The shape information discussed in the previous chapter are considered as feature / histogram. In general, the shape information is in the form of a floating point representation explained in Rasmusson et al. 2009, Strom *et al.* 2008, Burtcher *et al.* 2007 & Gamito and Dias, 2004 and the normalized value is in the form of single-precision floating-point format of the IEEE 754 standard as shown in Figure 3.

For any CBIR system, searching the relevant images from a large database is a tedious process. Such linear search may not manage the large database, as the database is growing day by day. Hence, to avoid the linear search process, suitable indexing scheme is used. The trivial bins of the shape feature are removed to reduce their dimension. The bins having four digits after the decimal points are truncated. Apart from this, the bins having 0 values and the bins having four 0's after the decimal point are also removed. As a result, the dimension of features is reduced to great extent having only non-zero bins. As each feature represents the shape information of the individual image, the

Figure 2. Schematic diagram of encoding and indexing

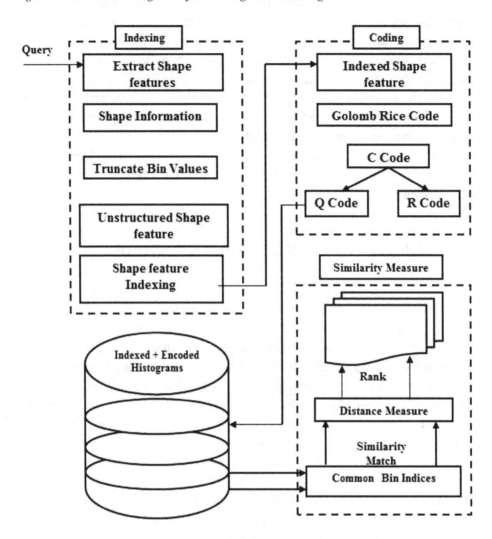

Figure 3. 32-bit IEEE floating-point representation

presence of unequal non-zero bins results in the structural variation of the histogram and is shown in Figure 4.

Figure 4. Structural variation of the reduced histogram

1	2	3	4	5	6	……………………………………	61	62	63	64
√			√	√				√	√	
		√			√		√			√
√	√			√				√	√	
	√				√		√		√	√

Since, the histogram bins are normalized, the floating point values are converted as integer without losing information. This is done since, GR coding uses integer values. Here, a suitable multiplication factor (Multi-Fact) is calculated by counting number of zero's after the decimal point to convert floating point values to integer values. Here, Multi-Fact is chosen as 1000 since, more bin values are having two 0's after the decimal point. Table 6 represents the Multi-Fact used in this chapter and the entire bin values of the histograms are converted into integer values. Thus, the obtained integer histogram values can now be used for indexing.

The representation of original shape and reduced shape feature is shown in the form of sparse matrix. Figure 5 represents the original normalized shape feature and Fig 5 *(b)* represents the reduced shape feature, which gives the effect of feature dimension reduction of feature vector thereby encouraging increased retrieval speed.

Figure 6 *(a)* represents shape information for a sample image and Figure 6 *(b)* represents its normalized shape information while the Fig 6 *(c)* represents encoded shape feature in the combined code format. The difference between original and reduced shape feature is found to be negligible.

The *Equation* (6) represents the indexing scheme (C_m) with 8 index levels (*m*) having different dimensions at each level.

Table 6. Multi-fact values based on the number of zero after the decimal point

No. of Zeros After Decimal Point	Multi-Fact
0.0	100
0.00	1000
0.000	10000

Figure 5. Sparse matrix representation (a) original shape feature (b) reduced shape feature

a

$$\begin{pmatrix} 0.5418 & 0.1043 & 0.2437 & 0.092 & 0.0043 & 0.0026 & 0.0011 & 0.0006 & 0.0003 \\ 0.0629 & 0.4843 & 0.2494 & 0.1101 & 0.0466 & 0.0214 & 0.0128 & 0.0076 & 0 \\ 0 & 0 & 0 & 0.0002 & 0.0008 & 0.6201 & 0.3403 & 0.0013 & 0 \\ 0 & 0 & 0 & 0 & 0.0001 & 0.0014 & 0.0714 & 0.6814 & 0.2222 \\ 0 & 0 & 0.0001 & 0.0004 & 0.0072 & 0.1134 & 0.6918 & 0.0925 & 0.0009 \end{pmatrix}$$

b

$$\begin{pmatrix} 541 & 104 & 243 & 92 & 4 & 2 & 1 & & \\ 62 & 484 & 249 & 110 & 46 & 21 & 12 & 7 & \\ & & & & & 620 & 340 & 1 & \\ & & & & & 1 & 71 & 681 & 222 \\ & & & & 7 & 113 & 691 & 92 & \end{pmatrix}$$

$$C_m = \left[1 + (IF) * (m - 1) \leq R_m \leq (IF) * m \right] \qquad (6)$$

In the above Equation, *IF* represents Index Factor=8, R_m is feature dimension range and m is the index level [1-8]. A sample indexing structure with the shape feature dimension range is depicted in Table 7. In this chapter, the value of *m* and *IF* is fixed based on exhaustive retrieval experiments only. For instance, the histogram having 15 bins fit in index 2, since it falls in the dimension range of [9-16].

The entire image database is grouped into several small blocks. For a given query image, the features are extracted, pre-processed, dimension is reduced and compared with the images in the matched block in lesser time.

Each block index has their header value in the form of *M*-parameter for which the encoding and decoding offset are calculated. The value of *M* for each block is calculated adaptively based on the indexed block size. The histogram blocks indexing works well even with uncontrolled data set of WWW. The indexing technique can find out the ground truth of images easily for each block. Thus, considering the ground truth of each block index, the *M*-parameter is calculated using *Equation* (7).

Figure 6. Pictorial representation of original histogram and various code formats histogram (a) sample image (b) normalized shape information (c) encoded shape information

a

b

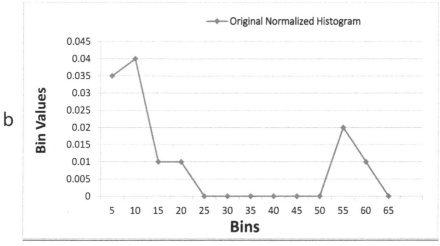

c

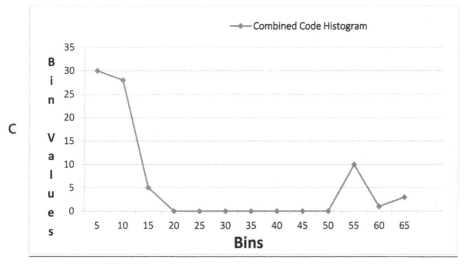

Table 7. Sample indexing structure

Index	Histogram Dimension	Range	M-Parameter
1	8	[1-8]	108
2	16	[9-16]	82
3	24	[17-24]	74
4	32	[25-32]	63
5	40	[33-40]	44
6	48	[41-48]	32
7	56	[49-56]	25
8	64	[57-64]	12

$$M = \sum_{i=1}^{n} \left[\left(\frac{h_i}{n} \right) * W \right] \tag{7}$$

In the above equation, W is constant parameter fixed to 0.69 (Zobel & Moffat, 2006), n is the total number of reduced histogram bins of respective block index, hi is the reduced histogram bin value of respective block, M is the tunable parameter for quotient and remainder encoding. The histogram bin values are in the form of integer N and are encoded using tunable parameter *M*. The bin values are divided into quotient *(Q)* and remainder *(R)* part using *Equation* (8) and *Equation* (9).

$$Quotient\,(Q) = \text{int}\,[N/M] \tag{8}$$

$$\text{Re}\,mainder\,(R) = [N \bmod M] \tag{9}$$

If power of *M* is 2, then rice code has to be applied to the remainder and $\lceil \log_2 (M) \rceil$ bits are needed for encoding. Alternatively, if *M* is not a power of 2, then *Equation* (10) is applied for encoding the remainder.

$$b = \lceil \log_2 (M) \rceil \tag{10}$$

While coding, two important conditions are noted as given below.

1. If $r < 2^b - M$ $r < 2^b - M$, code r in plain binary, using b-1 bits
2. If $r \geq 2^b - M$ $r \geq 2^b - M$, code the number $r + 2^b - M$ $r + 2^b - M$ in plain binary, using b bits.

Based on the quotient and remainder values, code words are generated as per code format given in *Equation* (11).

$$CodeFormat =< Quotient\, Code >< \mathrm{Re}\, mainder\, Code > \qquad (11)$$

The sample encoded histogram is shown in Table 8. The average bit length of the encoded histogram is calculated and it is found that the average bit length of the dimension reduced histogram is always low.

The various code formats such as *C Code*, *R Code* and *Q Code* are applied for a sample block index and used for the retrieval. The retrieval performance is tested for all the code formats and it is noticed that the retrieval performance of *Q Code* is same compared to *C Code*. The performance of *R Code* is poor due to the fact that it contains only minimum information. As a result, the *Q Code* information alone is sufficient to achieve good result and is considered equal to the *C Code* information. This is mathematically represented in terms of entropy in *Equation* (12).

$$E(C\ Code) = E\left(\left\langle Q\ Code\right\rangle\left\langle R\,Code\right\rangle\right)$$
$$= E\left(\left\langle Q\ Code\right\rangle\left\langle 0\right\rangle\right) \qquad (12)$$
$$E(C\,Code) \cong E\left(\left\langle Q\,Code\right\rangle\right)$$

Since <R Code> is negligible.

The entropy for C Code and Q Code for various images is calculated and it is noticed that the information content of C Code is slightly greater [w=0.1-0.4] compared to the Q Code and is shown in *Equation* (13). This is due to

Table 8 Encoded histogram block

Trunc- Histo	Final (MF)	Trunc*(MF)	M	Q	Q Code	R	R Code	Code
0.0028		2		0	0	2	0010	0010
0.005	1000	5	25	0	0	5	0101	0101

the fact that C Code includes both Q Code and R Code. Thus, the difference between the entropy of C Code and Q Code is very low and Q Code alone is sufficient for representing the histogram, thereby reducing the bit length.

$$E(C\,Code) \cong w * E(Q\,Code) \tag{13}$$

PERFORMANCE EVALUATION OF INDEXING SHAPE-PATTERN AND TEXTUAL FEATURE

Images from Corel database with 10,000 images having 100 categories are considered and the FOS feature of each image is treated as high dimensional data. The total number of vector is 10,000 (FOSV), the dimension of each FOSV is 7 (D) and the total (Ptotal) is 70000. As mentioned earlier, most of the bin values of FOSV may have values zero or close to zero. This is due to the fact that the bin value of square is high for a square dominant image and other bin values may be zero or approximately zero. The points with zero values are discarded and only PDist points are used to represent Ptotal and thereby the feature is represented in a compact form. The first K-dominant dimension of query vector is identified, pattern is created and the clusters related to those patterns are retained for computing the K-NN. For comparison, the FOS of Corel database is extracted and they are maintained both in the normal form and indexed form. Here, the normal form is referred to as the feature vector stored in a sequence form and the indexed form is referred to as the pattern based indexing structure. The performance is evaluated using Precision, Recall and F1 score. Precision is measured by retrieving the top-20 results for large number of queries and the average of the all the results is calculated. In Figure 7, the average precision is shown for various nearest neighbors. The average precision of Indexed FOS (IFOS) and Linear FOS (LFOS) are similar up to top-15 NN. For 20 NN, the precision of IFOS is slightly better than the LFOS and this is due to fact that the cluster pattern has effectively grouped the images for improving the Precision of retrieval. In addition, the higher Precision of retrieval is achieved by comparing lesser number of features, which has reduced the retrieval time.

In Figure 8, the average Recall for various NN is depicted. The result is interesting compared to the result given in Figure 7. The reason for performance enhancement is due to the capability of pattern based indexing scheme, where relevant images are grouped together effectively in a cluster, based on the shape categories. In addition, the F1 score is calculated and the result is presented in Figure 9. Based on all these experimental results, it is observed that the performance of the indexing approach is convincing as relevant images are indexed effectively using suitable pattern.

Performance Evaluation Using Both FOS Feature and Textual Information

The performance of this scheme is evaluated using uncontrolled database. Google (http://www.google.com) is a search engine with large number of indexed web pages and comparing the encoded scheme with Google is more practical than searching in small-scale. The encoded approach has generated uncontrolled dataset using Google. This is done using a crawler that fetches and saves both the HTML pages and its related images. The reason for using web documents and images from WWW is that text information is extracted for indexing purpose. In controlled image datasets, the text information may not be available for describing the image content. In contrast, the web document, in general uses text to describe the content of images. This is being considered as one of the primary reasons for using the crawled document. The terms

Figure 7. Average precision of retrieval

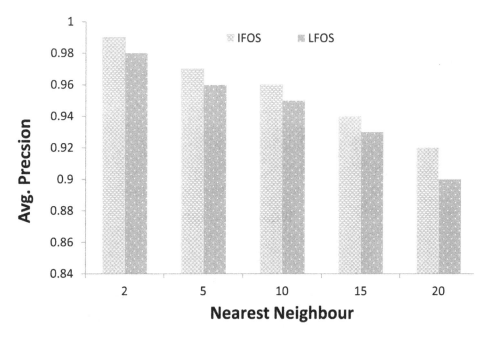

Figure 8. Average recall of retrieval

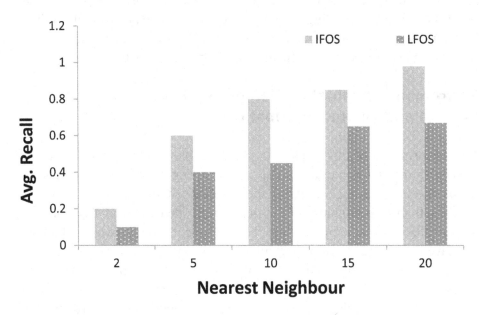

Figure 9. The average F1 score

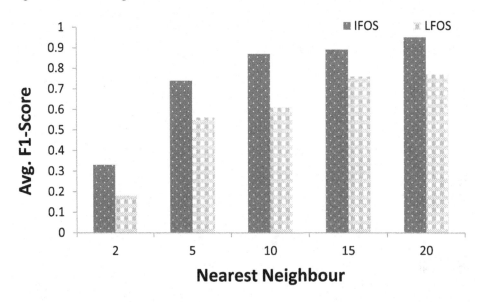

related to various shapes are provided as query to the Google system and only the top-100 links are considered for evaluation process. This collection contains at least one qualified image in each web page. The URL links are given as input to the crawler for fetching those particular pages. The web pages associated with each query are saved in a separate repository, where all web pages in the same repository are semantically related and relevant to the same topic. The aim is to evaluate and investigate retrieval approaches using this heterogeneous collection of web pages that are browsed by users with various information categories. The total number of web pages in the dataset is 10,00,000 that cover various topics of interest and each page includes the mixed and overlapping of text/ images.

For the experiment, the ground truth about Google search engine is not known and in the absence of ground truth, the only way to present the performance objectively is through Perceived Precision (PP), which is similar to Precision. The PP is measured by the person who is performing the queries. For a query, the person visually goes through the retrieval set by varying the NN. For each NN, the person finds out the relevant as well as irrelevant images and calculates PP. As mentioned in previous chapter, a group of post graduate students have performed the experiments and the Precision measured by the group is averaged and presented as result. Usually, online users are interested only in top-10 to top-100 web pages and PP is evaluated for these ranked web pages only. Since web pages contain text, images, etc., it is decided to evaluate the retrieval performance using text, FOS feature and combination of both.

The performance of text based retrieval using textual feature is shown in Figure 10. The PP for top 100 NN is presented from 10 NN. The average PP of the IFOS is encouraging compared to Google. The performance deficiency of Google lies in the fact that it displays information from all commercial and social network pages within the top-100. For instance, while providing the keywords in Google say "Shape of a ball", the content from social networking pages like Facebook and Google+ are displayed on top-100. However, the IFOS uses text information effectively, such that the relevant images alone are displayed on the top.

For image retrieval, Google Image search is used for comparison and its result is shown in Figure 11. The Google image search interface is used for image queries and the result is calculated. The same groups who have performed the text based query have performed this experiment also. It is observed from the Figure 11 that the performance of IFOS is good compared to Google system. The reason for the improved performance is that the Google uses text information alone for describing the image content and IFOS uses the FOS for describing the image content.

Figure 10. The average PP using textual feature as query

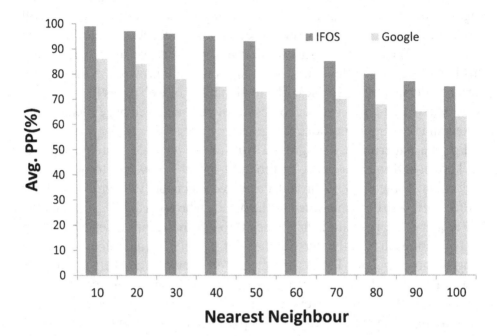

Finally, both the text and IFOS are combined together as query and the retrieval is shown in Figure 12. Here, only the performance of IFOS alone is presented and the reason is that there is no interface available to provide both the text and image feature in the Google system. Based on all the above results, it is observed that the performance of IFOS is better compared to the popular search engine system. The reason is that the pattern based indexing for both textual and low-level features identifies the relevant images effectively.

Performance Evaluation of Encoded FOS Feature

The effectiveness of the encoded histogram is evaluated in an image retrieval system. For experiment, MIT benchmark dataset with 9356 images is used in which 9144 object dominant images are categorized into 101 classes and 212 texture dominant images are categorized into 19 classes. Some query images from various classes are selected randomly for computing Recall and Precision and considered top 50 retrieval images. The similarity measure discussed in Chapter 5 is used as the distance metric to measure the distance between query and distance images and for original normalized histogram. The Recall vs. Precision is depicted in Figure 13 (a) and it is observed that

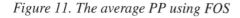

Figure 11. The average PP using FOS

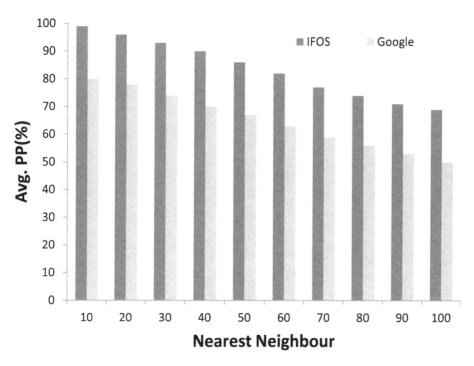

for lower values of Recall, the Precision is getting higher, which is reaching around 94%. The difference in Precision for various Recalls using encoded and original histogram is almost zero. Further to consolidate the performance of the encoded approach, the F-measure is calculated, which represents harmonic mean of Recall and precision. It can be noticed from the Figure 13(b) that the difference in F-Measure of encoded and original histogram for various nearest neighbours is almost zero. This performance enhancement is due to the fact that the encoding procedure just assigns the code for minimizing the size of the histogram and the information is not lost. Thus, it is noticed that the encoded feature performs well and retrieves the same result set as original histogram but consumes less space thereby reducing the retrieval time.

It is mentioned that the block indexed database gives better efficiency in retrieval time rather than flat database. Also, the entropy of Q Code and C Code are approximately same and as a result, Q Code alone is sufficient to represent the histogram. The performance comparison of Q Code and C Code histograms is evaluated using block indexed and flat indexed databases. These evaluations are carried out on MIT benchmark dataset and it contains 9144 object dominant images (101 classes) and 212 texture dominant images

Figure 12. The average PP for both text and FOS based query

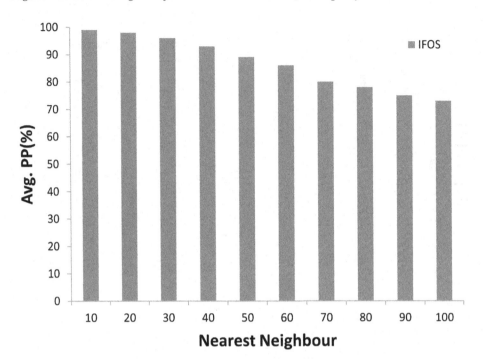

(19 classes). Here, the dataset is segregated as two database structures such as block indexing structure and flat database structure. The ground truth varies for both of these structures in calculating Recall. The way by which the images are grouped gives the ground truth for the block indexed database. For the flat database structure, MIT dataset structure and its classes that are predefined earlier are considered as the ground truth. The object and texture dominant images are randomly selected as query images. During retrieval, C Code histograms and Q Code histograms are considered individually for retrieving the images for a query. The performances of both C Code histograms and Q Code histograms on block and flat indexed databases are evaluated. The retrieval performance of both the encoded histograms is presented in Figure 14. Precision, Recall and F-measures are calculated for Q Code block, Q Code flat, C Code block and C Code flat. The retrieval result for p@2 is 99% for both C Code and Q Code block database and it is 95% for C Code and Q Code flat database. The C Code and Q Code result varies for p@5, 10, 15, 20, etc., for both database structures. It is observed from Figure 14(a), that the variation of C Code and Q Code in block database structure is low compared to flat one. The block database gives better result compared to

Figure 13. Performance between original and encoded histograms (a) precision vs. recall (b) F-measure

a

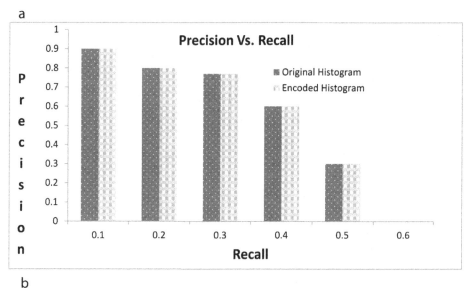

b

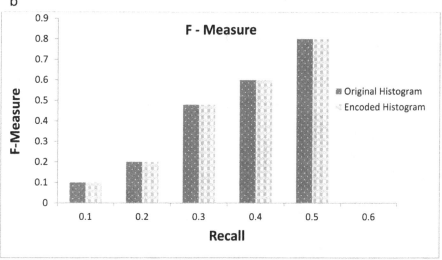

the flat database. Precision vs. Recall for Q Coded and C Coded histograms is considered for both database structures. Figure 14(b) represents average precision vs. Recall at 0.1, 0.15, 0.2, etc. Precision vs. Recall in block indexed structure gives encouraging results compared to the flat indexed structure.

Further, the Compression Ratio is estimated for various blocks. Table 9 indicates the Compression Ratio of 9144 object images from MIT dataset.

Figure 14. Retrieval performance of Q coded and C coded histograms using block indexed and flat database (a) precision (b)precision vs. recall

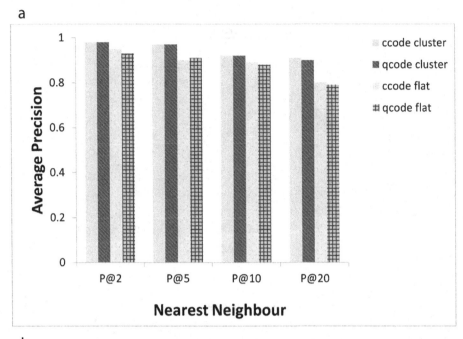

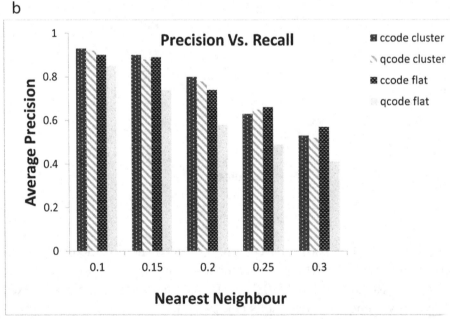

The objects based image histograms are grouped into various block indices depending on non-zero bin counts. The non-truncated histogram of respective blocks gives uncompressed histogram size and the truncated histogram bins gives compressed histogram size. The Compression Ratio is calculated for respective block indices using Equation (14).

$$C_R = \frac{Uncompressed \; image \; size}{Compressed \; image \; size} \tag{14}$$

Further, computation speed for various encoded formats are calculated and represented in Table 10. The disk computation speed is calculated in terms of time (sec) for object images. The computation speed is lesser for blocked structure when compared to unblocked structure. When it is measured with various code formats, Q Code block structure achieved lesser time compared to other coded formats.

The retrieval time of the encoded feature is compared with RLE as well as arithmetic encoding approaches [125]. In RLE approach, a rate-efficient codec is designed for tree-based retrieval and run length encoding is used.

Table 9. Compression ratio of object images from MIT dataset

Hist Block Index	Hist Block size= ∑(Hist)	Uncompressed Hist Bins size = ∑(Hist * 64)	Compressed Hist Bins size = ∑(Hist* Non-Zero bins)	Compression Ratio
1	98	6272	530	11.8
2	755	48320	10579	4.57
3	1948	124672	46284	2.69
4	2745	175680	88132	1.99
5	3598	230272	149008	1.55
		Avg = 117043	Avg = 58907	Avg = 1.98

Table 10. Computation speed for MIT dataset

Code Formats	Computation Speed (sec)
Q Code block indexed	3
Q Code flat indexed	5.13
C Code block indexed	8.16
C Code flat indexed	11.44

However, the approach had a limitation that runs length encoding is not able to work well at continuous-tone images. The other approach used for comparison is arithmetic coding and the images are divided into block based histograms. The maximum and minimum pixel value for the entire image is found for fixing a range (R). Further, block size (R× R) is set using contrast of the image for performing arithmetic coding. The performance measures for all the approaches are estimated in terms of Precision, Recall and F-measure and shown in Figure 15. The Precision is calculated and presented in Figure 15(a). This approach gives 97% and RLE approach gives 85% at p@2. Recall is calculated for the proposed approach and is represented in Figure 15 (b). Recall is 25% for proposed approach and 15% for a comparative approach for Recall at 0.1. It is 44% for proposed approach and 22% for a comparative approach for Recall at 0.2 and so on. Figure 15(c) represents Precision Vs. Recall for different query images. The ground truth and Precision vs. recall are taken individually for various blocks and then average Precision Vs. Recall is calculated. Proposed approach gives 70% and RLE approach gives 68% for Recall at 0.1. Figure 15(d) represents F-measure for various images. Proposed approach gives 18% and comparative approach gives 16%.

CONCLUSION

In general, content based image retrieval techniques display a large number of images for user query. It is found to be tedious for displaying most relevant images on the top of the result. The recent retrieval and indexing approaches suffer from the issues of curse of dimensionality, overlapping of vectors, need of extra parameters for clustering and not supporting incremental indexing. In this chapter, an indexing approach is introduced without enduring the above specified issues. The presented indexing structure is dynamically rearranged based on the occurrences of pattern for merging the common patterns in low-level feature. While indexing, the dominant pattern in the feature is used as key and based on which all the similar features are grouped together. This encoding procedure allows the user to search only a portion of feature database and there by reduces the search time considerably. Further, the feature is encoded using GR coding scheme and the feature database space required is reduced considerably. While there are many encoding scheme available, in this chapter GR coding is used for simplicity and its applicability. During encoding process, it is found that the quotient code for GR coding scheme alone sufficient to capture the information content of feature without loss

Figure 15. Performance comparison of proposed and comparative approach (a) average precision (b) average recall (c) precision vs. recall (d) F1-measure

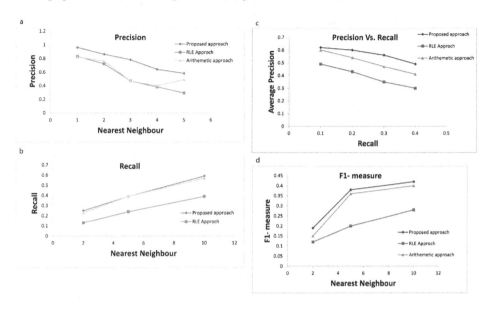

of important information. In line with previous chapters, the performance of the indexing and encoding scheme is evaluated using Precision, Recall and F1 Score. The Google is used as comparative system and found that the performance of encoded feature is good. In addition, the compression ratio obtained by the proposed scheme also discussed and numerical statistics is presented. Overall, the recommended indexing scheme reduces the search space by following predetermined pattern for clustering. The encoding scheme reduces the size of the feature database and also achieves good precision of retrieval.

REFERENCES

Ardizzoni, S., Bartolini, I., & Patella, M. (1999) Windsurf: Region-Based Image Retrieval Using Wavelets. *DEXA Workshop*, 167–173.

Barrios, J. M., Bustos, B., & Skopal, T. (2014). Analyzing and dynamically indexing the query set. *Information Systems, Elsevier Science.*, *45*, 37–47. doi:10.1016/j.is.2013.05.010

Burtscher, M., & Ratanaworabhan, P. (2007). High Throughput Compression of Double-Precision Floating-Point Data. *Proceedings of the Data Compression Conference (DCC '07)*. doi:10.1109/DCC.2007.44

Colombo, C., Bimbo, A. D., & Pala, P. (1999). Semantics in Visual Information Retrieval. *IEEE MultiMedia, 6*(3), 38–53. doi:10.1109/93.790610

Gamito, M. N., & Dias, M. S. (2004). Lossless Coding of Floating Point Data with JPEG 2000. *Proceedings of the Society for Photo-Instrumentation Engineers, 5558*, 276–287. doi:10.1117/12.564830

Golomb, S. W. (1966). Run-length encoding. *IEEE Transactions on Information Theory, 12*(3), 399–401. doi:10.1109/TIT.1966.1053907

Jurie, F., & Triggs, B. (2005). Creating efficient codebooks for visual recognition. *Proceedings of International Conference on Computer Vision*, 604-610.

Kaski, S., Kangas, J., & Kohonen, T. (1998) Bibliography of Self-Organizing Map (SOM). *Neural Computing Surveys*, 1981-1997.

Leibe, B., Mikolajczyk, K., & Schiele, B. (2006). Efficient clustering and matching for object class recognition. *Proceedings of the British Machine Vision Conference*, 789-798. doi:10.5244/C.20.81

Li, Q., Luo, S., & Shi, Z. (2009). Fuzzy aesthetic semantics description and extraction for art image retrieval. *Computers and Mathematics with Applications, Elsevier Science, 57*(6), 1000–1009. doi:10.1016/j.camwa.2008.10.058

Liu, M., & Yap, P.-T. (2012). Invariant representation of orientation fields for fingerprint indexing. *Pattern Recognition, Elsevier Science, 45*(7), 2532–2542. doi:10.1016/j.patcog.2012.01.014

Mejdoub, M., Fonteles, L., BenAmar, C., & Antonini, M. (2009). Embedded lattices tree: An efficient indexing scheme for content based retrieval on image databases. *Journal of Visual Communication and Image Representation, 20*(2), 145–156. doi:10.1016/j.jvcir.2008.12.003

Moosmann, F., Triggs, B., & Jurie, F. (2008). Randomized clustering forests for image classification. *IEEE Transactions on Pattern Analysis and Machine Intelligence, 30*(9), 1632–1646. doi:10.1109/TPAMI.2007.70822 PMID:18617720

Nister, D., & Stewenius, H. (2006) Scalable recognition with a vocabulary tree. *Proceedings of IEEE Conference on Computer Vision and Pattern Recognition*, 2161–2168. doi:10.1109/CVPR.2006.264

Poursistani, P., Nezamabadi-pour, H., Askari Moghadam, R., & Saeed, M. (2013). Image indexing and retrieval in JPEG compressed domain based on vector quantization. *Mathematical and Computer Modelling, Elsevier Science*, *57*(5/6), 1005–1017. doi:10.1016/j.mcm.2011.11.064

Qian, X., & Tagare, H. D. (2010). Adapting indexing trees to data distribution in feature spaces. *Journal of Computer Vision and Image Understanding*, *114*(1), 111–124. doi:10.1016/j.cviu.2009.07.002

Rasmusson, J., Strom, J., & Akenine-Moller, T. (2009). Error-bounded Lossy Compression of Floating-Point Colour Buffers using Quadtree Decomposition, The Visual Computer. *International Journal of Computer Graphics, Springer-Verlag*, *26*(1).

Rusinol, M., Borras, A., & Llados, J. (2010). Relational indexing of Vectorial primitives for symbol spotting in line-drawing images. *Pattern Recognition Letters, Elsevier Science*, *31*(3), 188–201. doi:10.1016/j.patrec.2009.10.002

St-Yves & Naselaris. (2017). The feature-weighted receptive field: an interpretable encoding model for complex feature spaces. *NeuroImage*. https://doi.org/10.1016/j.neuroimage.2017.06.035

Strom, J., Wennersten, P., Rasmusson, J., Hasselgren, J., Munkberg, J., Clarberg, P., & Akenine-Moller, P. T. (2008). Floating-point buffer compression in a unified codec architecture. *Proceedings of the 23rd ACM SIGGRAPH/EUROGRAPHICS, Symposium on Graphics Hardware*, 75–84.

Sui, C., Bennamoun, M., & Togneri, R. (2017). Deep Feature learning for dummies: A simple auto-encoder training method using Particle Swarm Optimisation. *Pattern Recognition Letters*, *94*, 75–80. doi:10.1016/j.patrec.2017.03.021

Zobel, J., & Moffat, A. (2006). Inverted files for text search engines. *ACM Computing Surveys*, *38*(2), 6, es. doi:10.1145/1132956.1132959

Chapter 5
Similarity Measure for Matching Fuzzy Object Shapes

ABSTRACT

In this chapter, the Common Bin Similarity Measure (CBSM) is introduced to estimate the degree of overlapping between the query and the database objects. All available similarity measures fail to handle the problem of Integrated Region Matching (IRM). The technical procedure followed for extracting the objects from images is well defined with an example. The performance of CBSM is compared with well-known methods and the results are given. The effect of IRM with CBSM is also proved by the experimental results. In addition, the performance of CBSM in encoded feature is compared with similar approaches. Overall, the CBSM is a novel idea and very much suitable for matching objects and ranking on their similarities.

INTRODUCTION

The strategy to estimate the fuzziness associated with the geometric and margin properties of objects in images to extract the Fuzzy Object Shape (FOS) is discussed in Chapter 3. A Fuzzy Object Level image matching algorithm is discussed for measuring the similarity between the query and database images. The working principle of similarity measure is explained in this chapter for measuring the degree of closeness of objects present in both query and database images. It is well-known fact that the similarity measure is an important component of retrieval systems. The existing similarity

DOI: 10.4018/978-1-5225-3796-0.ch005

measures typically define some meaning of similarity and propose algorithms for computing it. The meaning of similarity is application dependent, and should only be determined by the user. Therefore, there is a need for a generic approach where users can define the meaning of similarity. A parameterized similarity operator is proposed based on the time warped edit distance, where the meaning of similarity is generic and left for user to define (Magdy, Sakr, & El-Bahnasy, 2017).

An approach is proposed to enhance the Resource-Allocation (RA) similarity in resource transfer equations of diffusion-like models, by giving a tunable exponent to the RA similarity and traversing the value of this exponent to achieve the optimal recommendation results (An et al., 2016). The Mnemonic Similarity Task (MST), has ability to recognize an item as distinct from one that was similar, but not identical to one viewed earlier. A growing body of evidence links these behavioral changes to age-related alterations in the hippocampus. It is found that while there was an age-related impairment on lure discrimination performance for both objects and scenes, relationships to brain volumes and other measure of memory performance were stronger when using objects. In particular, lure discrimination performance for objects showed a positive relationship with the volume of the hippocampus, specifically the combined dentate gyrus (DG) and CA3 subfields, and the subiculum (Stark & Stark, 2017). Relational reasoning is sophisticated cognition in humans is discussed in Christie et al. (2016) and relational similarity is discussed without competing object matches both children and Pan Species.

FUZZY OBJECT LEVEL (FOL) SIMILARITY MEASURE

The procedure for obtaining the objects in images is shown in Figure 1. A similar traditional method, say, connected component detection is based on graph theory principle and the connected components are uniquely labelled for a given heuristic. Once the first pixel of a connected component is found, all the connected pixels of the connected component are labelled and the next pixel is considered. Data structures such as linked list or queue is required for processing the labelled pixels.

In this work, Canny edge detection is used along with the morphological operations, Dilation and Close with appropriate parameter using MATLAB tool. It is well-known that the Canny edge detection algorithm is an optimal edge detector and its error rate is very low. It is important that the edges occurring in images should not be missed and that response of non-edges should be very low with localization of edge points. The Canny operator always tries to minimize the distance between the estimated edge pixels and the actual edge with one response to a single edge. However, it is very difficult to completely eliminate the possibility of multiple responses to an edge. This issue has been handled by the Canny edge detector by smoothing the images to eliminate the noise and to find the image gradient to highlight regions with high spatial derivatives. The algorithm then tracks along these regions and suppresses any pixel that is not at the maximum and the gradient array is now further reduced by hysteresis. The hysteresis is used to track along the remaining pixels that have not been suppressed and two thresholds are used for edge detection. Because of the above mentioned procedural advantages, an optimal edge detector, the Canny edge detection algorithm is used. This mechanism substantially reduces the computational time and improves the performance.

During the process, the input image is converted as gray image over which the Canny edge detection algorithm is applied. The Canny filter significantly reduces the amount of data in an image, while preserving the structural properties to be used for further processing. The MATLAB tool is used for carrying out both Canny edge detection and morphological operations. The edge function in MATLAB is used, which automatically find low and high values of the threshold. This value is relative to the highest value of the gradient magnitude of the image so that the manual intervention for each and every image is avoided. The default sigma of the function is sqrt (2). The output of the Canny shows lines of high contrast in the image. These lines do not adequately delineate the outline of the object of interest. While comparing with the original image, gaps in the lines surrounding the object in the gradient mask are predominant. These linear gaps are handled by dilating the linear structuring elements, which are created with the strel function. In this work, se90 = strel ('line', 3, 90) and se0 = strel ('line', 3, 0) are used. Here, se90 and se0 refers to the structuring element used in MATLAB. As a result, the binary gradient mask is dilated using the vertical structuring element followed by the horizontal structuring element. Finally, the close and fill functions are used for filling the hole to obtain a clear object. The entire procedure is depicted in Figure 1 and a sample input and output images are shown in Figure 2.

While calculating the value of minimum and maximum radius as well as other values from the objects, the centroid is considered as a reference measure

Figure 1. Block diagram of object extraction from images

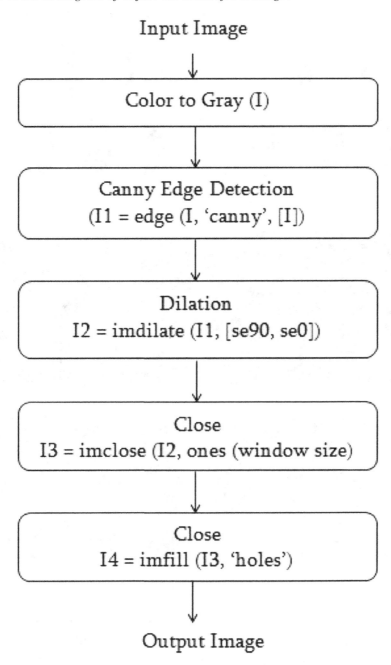

from which the relative values are calculated. As a result, the range of values is [0-1] and the defined equations from 1 to 7 are invariant to rotation, scaling

Figure 2. Pictorial View of object extraction from images (a) original image sample (b) gray scale image (c) edge detection (d-e-f) result of morphological operation

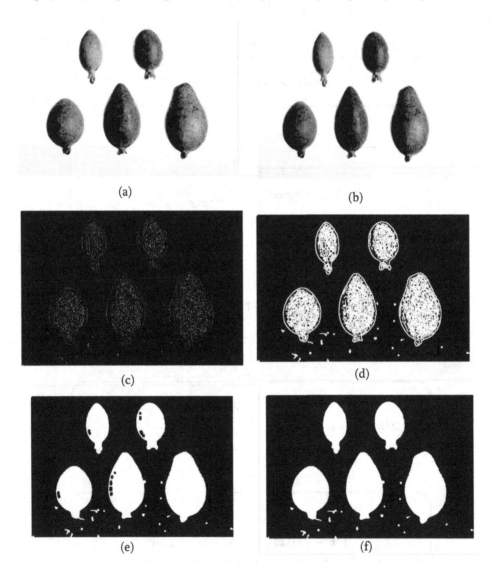

(a)

(b)

(c)

(d)

(e)

(f)

and translation. In addition, the smaller sized objects are not considered for finding the distance between two objects as their contribution is very small. Finally, the image is represented as a set of n non-overlapping partitions as follows:

$$I \equiv \left\{ FO_1 \mid FO_2 \mid FO_3 \mid .... \mid FO_n \right\}$$ (1)

Here, n is the number of fuzzy objects in an image, each FO_i is the fuzzy object and they are represented by feature vector and is denoted as follows.

$$FO_i \equiv \left\{ FC, FE, FS, FR, FRh, FCo, FCy \right\} \tag{2}$$

Using this equation, the values of fuzzy circle, ellipse, square, rectangle, rhombus, cone and cylinder are captured and are represented as feature vector. In addition, the centroid and the size of each fuzzy object is stored separately. Thus, each image is decomposed as fuzzy-object and represents the fuzzy object-level information. Similarity between fuzzy-objects in the database (D) and query image (Q) is calculated by comparing feature vector, size and position of the objects. Let us consider two images Q and D containing $n1$ and $n2$ number of fuzzy-objects, respectively. The objects present in both the images may be represented as $FOQ_1, FOQ_2, FOQ_3, ..., FOQ_{n1}$ and $FOD_1, FOD_2, FOD_3, ..., FOD_{n2}$ respectively. It is assumed that the objects of the image Q, i.e., $FOQ_1, FOQ_2, FOQ_3, ..., FOQ_{n1}$ are sorted in descending orderofitssizedenotedas $S\left(FOQ_i \right), i = 1, 2, ... n_1$ suchthat $S(FOQ_k) >= S(FOQ_m)$ for $k < m$. The size (area) of the objects is calculated based on the number of pixels in a respective object. A standard approach for matching objects between two images is the Integrated Region Matching (IRM) method (Wang et al. 2000; Magdy, 2017). In this method, each object of one image is matched with each object of the second image. However, the averaging effect matches two completely dissimilar images during retrieval. The similarity between two images can be measured as the degree of match between their objects. The complete algorithm for Fuzzy Object Level Image Matching is shown below:

In the above algorithm, the value of dist_threshold is 25% of the distance between the FOQ and FOD, 75% of the difference between the centroid of FOQ and FOD is set as cent_threshold and 75% max_overlap is considered.

In Figure 3(a) and 3(b), sample query and database image with objects are shown. Initially, the objects in both the query and database images are sorted based on their size. Each object in the query image is matched with the objects in the database image, based on their feature similarity and as a result, the closest object combination is obtained. Then, the objects in the database image are sorted, based on their feature distance value and the degree of overlap is being calculated based on their center. Out of all the candidate objects of database image, only those objects whose centers are close to the

Algorithm 1. Fuzzy Object Level Image Matching Algorithm

Input: Query Image Q
Output: Similar Output Images
    1. Consider Query Image Q and Database Image D
    2. Simi-Q-D ← 0.0,
        matched_FOQ$_i$ ← 0.0,
        matched_FOD$_i$ ← 0.0,
        max_match ← 0.9,
        overlap ← 0.9,
        max_overlap ← 1.0
3. n1 ← Number of fuzzy-Objects in Q
4. n2 ← Number of fuzzy-Objects in Q

5. Sort $FOQ_1, FOQ_2, FOQ_3, ..., FOQ_{n1}$ in descending order of their size

6. Sort $FOD_1, FOD_2, FOD_3, ..., FOD_{n2}$ in descending order of their size
    7. For Each fuzzy-object in FOD$_i$
        Calculate feature_dist (FOQ$_i$, FOD$_j$)
        Sort the fuzzy_objects in D based on feature_dist in descending order

Let the sorted fuzzy object in D be $FOD_1, FOD_2, FOD_3, ..., FOD_{n2}$

    8. For Each fuzzy-object in Q
        For Each fuzzy-object in D
    if (matched_FOQi < max_match ← 0.0, && matched_FODj <max_match)
        if(feature_dist (FOQ$_i$, FOD$_j$) < dist_threshhold)
        if(cent (FOQ$_i$, FOD$_j$) < cent_threshhold)
        if(overlap< max_overlap)

$$matched\_FOQ_i = matched\_FOQ_i + \frac{(1 - matched\_FOD_j) * S(FOD_j)}{\left(S(FOQ_i)\right)}$$

else
matched_FOD$_j$ = 0

$$matched\_FOD_j = matched\_FOD_j + \frac{(1 - matched\_FOQ_i) * S(FOD_i)}{\left(S(FOQ_i)\right)}$$

$matched\_FOQ_i = 0$
Simi-Q-D = Simi-Q-D + matched_FOQ$_i$ * S(FOD$_j$)
Return (Simi-Q-D)

---

center of objects in the query image are considered. This is done to ensure that the two distinctly different objects having the same features are not matched with one another. Thus, such two objects are considered for matching only if their centers are less than the cent_threshold. Further, if an object of database image is already matched with an object of query image, it is not considered again for matching with another object of the query image. However, if an object of database image is partially matched with an object of query image, the remaining part is considered for matching with another object of the

Figure 3. Illustration of Overlap Matching Object (a) Objects in a Sample Query Image (b) Objects in a Sample Database Image

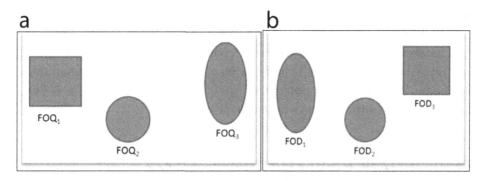

query image. Similarly, an object of query image may be matched with more than one object of database image through partial matching with each one of them. In the algorithm, any object of query image, which is matched, with objects of database image by a fraction of max_match or more, is considered to be matched. This is done because two objects cannot always be matched exactly due to small camera movement or light variations. A typical value of max_match is 90%.

The illustration of the matching procedure is presented below. The objects in query and database images are sorted based in its size and the ordered sequence of objects are as follows:

$$S(FOQ_2) < S(FOQ_1) < S(FOQ_3)$$

$$S(FOD_2) < S(FOD_1) < S(FOD_3)$$

The procedure for calculating the feature distance between the fuzzy objects is shown as follows:

$$feature\_dist(FOQ_2, FOD_2) = (circle, circle) = 0.0$$

$$feature\_dist(FOQ_2, FOD_3) = (circle, square) = 0.8$$

$$feature\_dist(FOQ_2, FOD_1) = (circle, ellipse) = 0.7$$

$$feature\_dist(FOQ_1, FOD_2) = (square, circle) = 0.8$$

feature_dist(FOQ$_1$,FOD$_3$)=(square, square)=0.0

feature_dist(FOQ$_1$,FOD$_1$)=(square, ellipse)=0.6

The above procedure is further preceded for rest of the objects and the feature distance is calculated and for want of space only six combinations are presented. Now, the fuzzy objects are sorted based on feature_dist as FOD$_2$, FOD$_3$, FOD$_1$ and the degree of overlap is calculated.

PERFORMANCE EVALUATION OF FUZZY OBJECT LEVEL MATCHING

The objects present in the images are extracted and for each object, the membership value is calculated to construct feature vector. The closeness of the object of interest with circle, ellipse, square, rectangle, rhombus, cone and cylinder is obtained. For all the database images, the membership values are calculated and stored in feature database. Given a query image, the feature is extracted and compared with the features in the feature database and ranked. The performance of the proposed approach is evaluated using standard performance metrics such as Precision, Recall and coefficient of variation.

Based on the results presented in Table 1, using various controlled databases, it is noticed that the Fuzzy Object Shape along with the similarity

Table 1. Recall vs. mean precision on University of Washington (UW) dataset

Approaches	Recall									
	0.1	0.2	0.3	0.4	0.5	0.6	0.7	0.8	0.9	1.0
FOSIR	**0.82**	**0.80**	**0.78**	**0.75**	**0.74**	**0.73**	**0.72**	**0.71**	**0.70**	**0.69**
Chahooki and Charkari	0.78	0.77	0.75	0.73	0.71	0.68	0.65	0.63	0.62	0.60
Ayed *et al*	0.76	0.75	0.73	0.72	0.70	0.68	0.65	0.64	0.62	0.60
Li *et al*	0.70	0.69	0.68	0.65	0.63	0.61	0.60	0.59	0.58	0.56
Zagoris *et al*	0.77	0.76	0.75	0.73	0.71	0.70	0.68	0.67	0.66	0.64
Patrizio and Claudia	0.80	0.79	0.78	0.76	0.73	0.71	0.70	0.68	0.66	0.64
Tran *et al*	0.80	0.78	0.77	0.75	0.73	0.72	0.70	0.69	0.65	0.64
Hasegawa and Tabbone	0.79	0.77	0.76	0.74	0.72	0.70	0.69	0.68	0.66	0.67
Deng *et al*	0.80	0.79	0.77	0.76	0.75	0.71	0.70	0.69	0.67	0.66
Tanács *et al*	0.80	0.79	0.77	0.73	0.72	0.71	0.70	0.69	0.68	0.67

measure outperforms all the other similar approaches. This is due to the fact that most of the images contain object level information, which can be used as feature for discriminating one from another. The presented Fuzzy Object Shape based representation scheme effectively captures the object information using a suitable fuzzy membership function with minimum and maximum radii values. The extracted values effectively discriminated the query object with the database object. Also, the proposed similarity measure complements the feature vector and removes the averaging effect by IRM. The similarity between the objects is calculated by considering the feature distance and centroid and thus, most of the relevant images are placed at the top of the retrieval set. Further, while observing the result presented in Table 1, FOSIR achieves lower Precision for various Recall. This is due to the fact that these image datasets contain images without clear boundaries. All these images are natural scenery and thus, objects overlap with each other, which influence the result.

In addition to all the above results on controlled database, it is also important to evaluate the performance of FOSIR in an uncontrolled image data set. The proposed approach have crawled 40,000 images from the Internet and created a feature database. Since there is no possibility to measure the ground truth, only Precision is used as evaluation parameter and the same student group has performed the query and thus the Precision is calculated. The relevant image in the retrieval set is identified by the user who is performing the search and the same team is used for calculating the Precision for 1000 queries. The Precision is calculated for the NN 2, 5, 10, 15 and 20 and presented below in Table 2. It is observed that the Precision value of Chahooki and Charkari (2012), Ayed *et al.* (2012), Li *et al.* (2009), Zagoris *et al.* (2011) and Patrizio and Claudia (2013) is in similar range and the Precision of Patrizio and Claudia (2013) is higher than all of these methods. Tran *et al.* (2014), Hasegawa and Tabbone (2014), Deng *et al.* (2014) and Tanács *et al.* (2015) are maintaining a range and however, the performance of FOSIR is encouraging when compared with all these methods and thus, Precision is higher than all the comparative methods.

Further, the performance of the proposed object based similarity measure is evaluated on the above uncontrolled database and is compared with IRM approach. The Precision is shown below in Table 3 and it is observed from the result that the performance of the proposed similarity measure is high (around 20% - 30%) compared to IRM. This improvement is due to the fact that the proposed object based similarity measure minimizes the averaging effect.

Table 2. Precision on uncontrolled database of 40,000 images

Approaches	Nearest Neighbour				
	P @2	P @5	P@10	P@15	P@20
FOSIR	**0.975**	**0.96**	**0.95**	**0.94**	**0.93**
Chahooki and Charkari (2012)	0.85	0.84	0.82	0.81	0.79
Ayed *et al.*(2012)	0.82	0.80	0.79	0.78	0.77
Li *et al.* (2009)	0.89	0.87	0.86	0.84	0.82
Zagoris *et al.*(2011)	0.88	0.87	0.85	0.83	0.82
Patrizio and Claudia (2013)	0.91	0.89	0.87	0.86	0.85
Tran *et al.*(2014)	0.90	0.89	0.87	0.85	0.84
Hasegawa and Tabbone (2014)	0.91	0.89	0.87	0.85	0.83
Deng *et al.* (2014)	0.92	0.90	0.88	0.86	0.84
Tanács *et al.* (2014)	0.93	0.91	0.89	0.88	0.86

A sample output for some of the query images are presented below in Figure 4, in which a sample output from the retrieval system for some object dominant query images is presented. In Figure 4 (a) and (b) the object dominant query image and the extracted object are presented. Similarly, Figure 4 (c) and (d) depict another original and object dominant image from the database. It is noticed that most of the images are relevant to the query image in terms of their object content. This is in contrast to the color based retrieval system, where the color content in the images is prominent and the human eye is influenced by the same. Further, it is known that object-based retrieval system retrieves set of images, which are closer to the query image in terms of object content. More results can, indeed, be provided through for want of space and clarity, only the following results are presented.

Table 3. Performance comparison of proposed object based similarity measure and IRM on uncontrolled database of 40,000 images

Approaches	Nearest Neighbour				
	P @2	P @5	P@10	P@15	P@20
Proposed Object Based Similarity Measure	**0.975**	**0.96**	**0.95**	**0.94**	**0.93**
IRM (Wang *et al.* 2000)	0.78	0.75	0.70	0.67	0.61

Figure 4. Sample output from the retrieval system for some query images (object dominant) (a)-(f): sample retrieval set along with extracted object

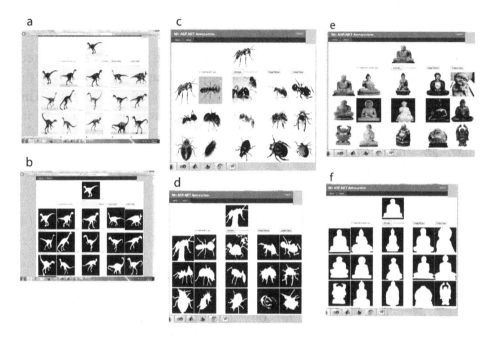

COMMON BINS SIMILARITY MEASURE (CBSM)

The conventional distance measures face the curse of dimensionality issue due to nearest-neighbor search. A Common Bins Similarity Measure is proposed, which achieve good response time without affecting the Precision. The entire database image is split into various blocks and indexed as $DB = (B1, B2, ..., Bm)$. The block contains unstructured image histograms with non-zero bins and represented as $Bm = (h1, h2, h3, ..., hk)$. The histogram bin is represented as $hk (Nj)$, such that Nj represents the bin value for the bin index j where $j=(1, 2, 3, ...)$. Given a query $hq(Ni)$, the matching Block Index$(B1, B2, ..., Bm)$ is identified using its histogram dimension range $(R1, R2, ..., Rm)$. The CBSM computes the distance between query histogram (hq) and histogram (hk) in matched block database. Since, there exist a structural variation in the histograms, the similarity approach considers common bins of the histogram to compute the distance between them. The non-zero bin counts of query $(count\_q)$ and block database histogram $(count\_k)$ are considered. The common bins $(Common(q))$ between hq and hk are identified and degree of common bins $(Common(Degree))$ is computed using Equation 3.

$$Common_{(Degree)} = \left| \frac{Common_{(q)}}{(Count\_q)} \right| \tag{3}$$

The common bin values of both the histograms (hq and hk) are compared. As the bits are binary, XOR logic is used for comparison, which gives the difference in the Common bin values (CB(diff)) for complete histogram. This is represented in Equation 4) and where, Ni(hq)represents the value of ith bin index of query histogram (hq) and Nj(hk) is the value of jth bin index of clustered database histogram (hk) which are common (i==j) where, i=(1,2, 3,....,n) and j=(1,2,3,...,n).

$$CB_{(diff)} = CB_{(diff)} + \sum_{i=j=1}^{n} \left(N_i^{(h_q)} - N_j^{(h_k)} \right) \tag{4}$$

In Table 4, sample hq and hk are presented for better understanding of the working principle of CBSM. The non-zero bins of both the histograms are counted and analyzed and it is observed that only five bins are common between them which are considered for calculating the similarity. The Common(Degree) of query histogram is computed using Equation 6). The encoded values (Q Code) of common bins of both histograms are compared and represented as CB(diff) using Equation 7).

Similarly, Common(Degree)and CB(diff) between query hq and all the other histograms (h1, h2, h3,…,hk) in the Block Bm are calculated. The CB(diff)(dist)is calculated by counting the number of 1's in CB(diff) of the histograms as shown in Equation 5).

$$CB_{(diff)}(dist) = CB_{(diff)}(Number of 1's) \tag{5}$$

Table 4. Comparison of encoded values between query and clustered database histogram

Common$_{(q)}$	count_q	Common$_{(Degree)}$	h$_q$ <Q Code>	h$_k$ <Q Code>	XOR	CB$_{(diff)}$=$\sum$XOR
3			1110	110	1000	
4			1110	111110	110000	
5	23	5/(23)	11110	11111110	11100000	11111100
54			111110	110	111000	
55			1110	10	1100	

The Commom(Degree) and CB(diff)(dist) are normalized and their combined values give distance between hq and (h1, h2, h3,..., hk) of the Block Bm. This is represented in Equation 6.

$$CBSM = \left(CB_{(diff)}(dist) \quad + Common_{(Degree)} \right) \tag{6}$$

The CBSM approach between hq and other histograms (h1, h2, h, ..., hk) of Bm is presented in Table 5 for better understanding. The CBSM ranges between [0-1] where, 0 denotes the closeness between hq and hk and vice versa.

PERFORMANCE EVALUATION OF CBSM

Further, the Compression Ratio is estimated for various blocks. Table 6 indicates the Compression Ratio of 9144 object images from MIT dataset. The objects based image histograms are grouped into various block indices depending on non-zero bin counts. The non-truncated histogram of respective blocks gives uncompressed histogram size and the truncated histogram bins gives compressed histogram size. The Compression Ratio is calculated for respective block indices using Equation 7).

$$CR = \frac{Uncompressed\ image\ size}{compressed\ image\ size} \tag{7}$$

Further, computation speed for various encoded formats are calculated and represented in Table 7. The disk computation speed is calculated in terms of time (sec) for object images. The computation speed is lesser for blocked

Table 5. CBSM between query and block indexed database histograms

B_m	$CB_{(diff)}$	$CB_{(diff)}^{(dist)}$	Normalized $CB_{(diff)}^{(dist)}$	$Common_{(Degree)}$	Normalized $Common_{(Degree)}$	$CBSM_{(Norm)}$
h_1	11111100	6	0.42	5/23=0.217	0.128	0.548
h_2	1100	2	0.14	8/23=0.347	0.204	0.344
h_3	1111000	4	0.28	11/23=0.478	0.282	0.562
h_4	111000	3	0.21	15/23=0.652	0.384	0.594
		=14		=1.694		

Table 6. Compression ratio of object images from MIT dataset

Hist Block Index	Hist Block size= ∑(Hist)	Uncompressed Hist Bins size = ∑(Hist * 64)	Compressed Hist Bins size = ∑(Hist* Non-Zero bins)	Compression Ratio
1	98	6272	530	11.8
2	755	48320	10579	4.57
3	1948	124672	46284	2.69
4	2745	175680	88132	1.99
5	3598	230272	149008	1.55
		Avg = 117043	Avg = 58907	Avg = 1.98

structure when compared to unblocked structure. When it is measured with various code formats, Q Code block structure achieved lesser time compared to other coded formats.

The retrieval time of the proposed approach is compared with RLE as well as arithmetic encoding approaches (Schindler, 1998). In RLE approach, a rate-efficient codec is designed for tree-based retrieval and run length encoding is used. However, the approach had a limitation that runs length encoding is not able to work well at continuous-tone images. The other approach used for comparison is arithmetic coding and the images are divided into block based histograms. The maximum and minimum pixel value for the entire image is found for fixing a range (R). Further, block size (R× R) is set using contrast of the image for performing arithmetic coding. The performance measures for all the approaches are estimated in terms of Precision, Recall and F-measure and shown in Figure The Precision is calculated and presented in Figure 5 (a). Proposed approach gives 97% and RLE approach gives 85% at p@2. Recall is calculated for the proposed approach and is represented in Figure 5 (b). Recall is 25% for proposed approach and 15% for a comparative approach for Recall at 0.1. It is 44% for proposed approach and 22% for a comparative approach for Recall at 0.2 and so on. Figure 5 (c) represents Precision Vs.

Table 7. Computation speed for MIT dataset

Code Formats	Computation Speed (sec)
Q Code block indexed	3
Q Code flat indexed	5.13
C Code block indexed	8.16
C Code flat indexed	11.44

Figure 5. Performance comparison of proposed and comparative approach (a) average precision (b) average recall (c) precision vs. recall (d) F1-measure

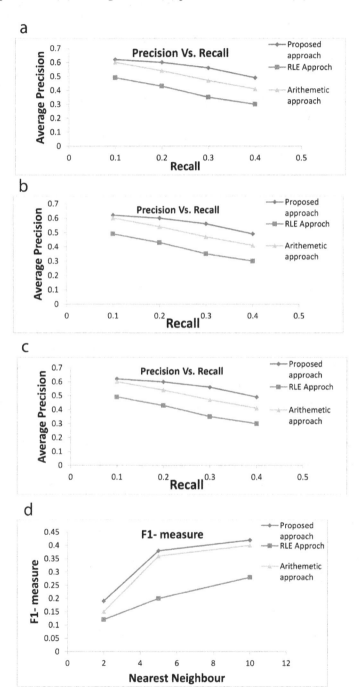

Recall for different query images. The ground truth and Precision vs. recall are taken individually for various blocks and then average Precision Vs. Recall is calculated. Proposed approach gives 70% and RLE approach gives 68% for Recall at 0.1. Figure 5 (d) represents F-measure for various images. Proposed approach gives 18% and comparative approach gives 16%. Figure 5 represents the retrieval result for the proposed approach and comparative approaches. It is noticed that the proposed approach shows 100% Precision, RLE approach gives 60% and arithmetic coding gives 80% result.

Thus, the proposed approach encourages good precision of retrieval apart from reduced bit length, retrieval time and computation speed compared to other similar approaches.

CONCLUSION

In this chapter, the CBSM is proposed to estimate the degree of overlapping between the query and the database objects. The importance of object based similarity is highlighted using review material. Almost all the available similarity measure fail to handle the problem of integrated region matching aspects. The technical procedure followed for extracting the objects from images is presented with an example. The matching procedure is explained and made it simple for the reader with a classical example. The performance of CBSM is compared with well-known methods and the result are presented. The performance result is presented and discussed for both controlled bench mark dataset and uncontrolled data set. The effect of IRM with CBSM is also proved by the experimental results. In addition, the performance of CBSM in encoded feature and compared with similar approaches. Overall, the CBSM is novel idea and very much suitable for matching objects and ranking on their similarities.

REFERENCES

An, Dong, Sun, Nie, & Fu. (2016). Diffusion-like recommendation with enhanced similarity of objects. *Physica A: Statistical Mechanics and its Applications, 461*(1), 708–715.

Ben Ayed, A., Kardouchi, S., & Selouani, S. A. (2012). Rotation invariant Fuzzy Shape Contexts based on Eigen shapes and Fourier transforms for efficient Radiological image retrieval. *Proceedings of International Conference on Multimedia Computing and Systems (ICMCS)*, 266–271.

Chahooki, M. A. Z., & Charkari, N. M. (2012) Supervised Shape Retrieval based on Fusion of Multiple Feature Spaces. *Proceedings of 20th Iranian Conference on Electrical Engineering (ICEE'12)*, 1072-1074. doi:10.1109/IranianCEE.2012.6292512

Christie, , Gentner, Call, Benjamin, & Haun. (2016). Sensitivity to Relational Similarity and Object Similarity in Apes and Children Current Biology. *Science Direct*, *26*(4), 531–535.

Deng, Z., Xiao, K., & Huang, J. (2014). A New Fuzzy Shape Context Approach Based on Multi-clue and State Reservoir Computing. *Proceedings of International Joint Conference on Neural Networks (IJCNN'14)*, 2361-2366. doi:10.1109/IJCNN.2014.6889800

Frosini, P., & Landi, C. (2013). Persistent Betti numbers for a noise tolerant shape based approach to image retrieval. *Pattern Recognition Letters*, *34*(8), 863–872. doi:10.1016/j.patrec.2012.10.015

Hasegawa, M., & Tabbone, S. (2014). Amplitude-only log Radon transform for geometric invariant shape descriptor. *Pattern Recognition, Elsevier Science*, *47*(2), 643–658. doi:10.1016/j.patcog.2013.07.024

Li, Q., Luo, S., & Shi, Z. (2009). Fuzzy aesthetic semantics description and extraction for art image retrieval. *Computers and Mathematics with Applications, Elsevier Science*, *57*(6), 1000–1009. doi:10.1016/j.camwa.2008.10.058

Magdy, N., Sakr, M. A., & El-Bahnasy, K. (2017). A generic trajectory similarity operator in moving object databases. *Egyptian Informatics Journal*, *18*(1), 29–37. doi:10.1016/j.eij.2016.07.001

Schindler, M. (1998). A Fast Renormalisation for Arithmetic Coding. *Proceedings of Data Compression Conference (DCC 98)*, 572.

Stark & Stark. (2017). Age-related deficits in the mnemonic similarity task for objects and scenes. Behavioural Brain Research, 333, 109-117.

Tanács, A., Lindblad, J., Sladoje, N., & Kato, Z. (2015). Estimation of linear deformations of 2D and 3D fuzzy objects. *Pattern Recognition, Elsevier Science, 48*(4), 1391–1403. doi:10.1016/j.patcog.2014.10.006

Tran, T. T., Pham, V. T., & Shyu, K. K. (2014). Image segmentation using fuzzy energy-based active contour with shape prior. *Journal of Visual Communication Image Representation, Elsevier Science, 25*(7), 1732–1745. doi:10.1016/j.jvcir.2014.06.006

Wang, J. Z., Li, J., & Wiederhold, G. (2000). SIMPLIcity: Semantics-sensitive Integrated Matching for Picture Libraries. *IEEE Transactions on Pattern Analysis and Machine Intelligence, 23*(9), 947–963. doi:10.1109/34.955109

Zagoris, K., Ergina, K., & Papamarkos, N. (2011). Image retrieval systems based on compact shape descriptor and relevance feedback information. *Journal of Visual Communication and Image Representation, Elsevier Science, 22*(5), 378–390. doi:10.1016/j.jvcir.2011.03.002

Chapter 6
Textual–Shape–Based Image Retrieval

ABSTRACT

In this chapter, a method to combine both text and image feature is considered. The FOS is explained in Chapter 3 is combined with textual information extracted (as discussed in Chapter 1). A clustering mechanism is formulated based on image, text and both. A retrieval is presented as an example to demonstrate the functionality by which the reader can understand the use of combining both textual keywords and FOS. The Chapter has consolidated the performance of combined feature using Precision, Recall and F1-score. The performance is evaluated and compared with well-known Google retrieved system.

INTRODUCTION

It has been observed that low-level features can be efficiently used to perform retrieval in domain-specific applications. Color histograms like Human Color Perception Histogram (HCPH) (Vadivel, Shamik & Majumdhar, 2008), (Deng 2001) & (Gevers & Stokman, 2004) and color-texture features like Integrated Color and Intensity Co-occurrence Matrix (ICICM) (Vadivel, Shamik & Majumdhar, 2007) and Fuzzy Object Shape (FOS) (Shanmugavadivu et al, 2015 & 2016) features show high precision of retrieval in such applications. However, in more generic applications, low-level features cannot always represent semantic content of images effectively. As a result, retrieval precision

DOI: 10.4018/978-1-5225-3796-0.ch006

tends to drop. It is observed that to use keywords to restrict the search space in such applications. For example, while searching for images on the World Wide Web (WWW), use of keywords may be quite helpful in filtering out web pages that are not relevant. In early years, textual keywords were used to be assigned by domain experts to images on the web, which made the annotations highly subjective. A survey of image retrieval systems for images available on the Internet may be found in TASI. Out of these image search engines, Google (www.google.com) consists of simple search options with a good advance search facility. It provides quick and reasonably good search results. Similar to Google, the search option of Yahoo (www.yahoo.com) is also simple. In addition, the performance of retrieval is quick, retrieved images are found to be relevant without dead links and duplicates.

Text in natural images is an important source of information, which can be utilized for many real-world applications, which focuses on a new problem say, distinguishing images that contain text from a large volume of natural images. To address this problem, multi-scale spatial partition network is proposed (Bai et al 2017). The network classifies images that contain text or not, by predicting text existence in all image blocks, which are spatial partitions at multiple scales on an input image. The whole image is classified as a text image as long as one of the blocks is predicted to contain text. The network classifies images very efficiently by predicting all blocks simultaneously in a single forward propagation.

An automatic image–text alignment algorithm is developed to achieve more effective indexing and retrieval of large-scale web images by aligning web images with their most relevant auxiliary text terms or phrases. (Zhou & Fan 2015). Initially, a large number of cross-media web pages are crawled and segmented into a set of image–text pairs the near-duplicate image clustering is used to group large-scale web images into a set of clusters of near-duplicate images according to their visual similarities. The near-duplicate web images in the same cluster share similar semantics and are simultaneously associated with a same or similar set of auxiliary text terms or phrases which co-occur frequently in the relevant text blocks, thus performing near-duplicate image clustering can significantly reduce the uncertainty on the relatedness between the semantics of web images and their auxiliary text terms or phrases. Finally, random walk is performed over a phrase correlation network to achieve more precise image–text alignment by refining the relevance scores between the web images and their auxiliary text terms or phrases.

Learning effective relevance measures plays a crucial role in improving the performance of content-based image retrieval systems. Despite extensive research efforts for decades, how to discover and incorporate semantic information of images still poses a formidable challenge to real-world CBIR systems. A hybrid textual-visual relevance learning method is proposed, which mines textual relevance from image tags and combines textual relevance and visual relevance for CBIR (Cui et al 2017). To alleviate the sparsity and unreliability of tags, tag completion is performed to fill the missing tags as well as correct noisy tags of images. Then, users' semantic cognition is captured to images by representing each image as a probability distribution over the permutations of tags. Finally, instead of early fusion, a ranking aggregation strategy is adopted to sew up textual relevance and visual relevance seamlessly.

Visual vocabulary is the core of the Bag-of-visual-words (BOW) model in image retrieval. In order to ensure the retrieval accuracy, a large vocabulary is always used in traditional methods. However, a large vocabulary will lead to a low recall. In order to improve recall, vocabularies with medium sizes are proposed, but they will lead to a low accuracy. To address these two problems, a new method for image retrieval is proposed based on feature fusion and sparse representation over separable vocabulary (Yanhong et al 2017).

Multimodal Retrieval is a well-established approach for image retrieval. Usually, images are accompanied by text caption along with associated documents describing the image. Textual query expansion as a form of enhancing image retrieval is a relatively less explored area. A study is presented to understand the effect of expanding textual query on both image and its associated text retrieval. It reveals that judicious expansion of textual query through key phrase extraction can lead to better results, either in terms of text-retrieval or both image and text-retrieval. To establish this, two well-known key phrase extraction techniques is used based on tf-idf and KEA. While query expansion results in increased retrieval efficiency, it is imperative that the expansion be semantically justified. So, a graph-based key phrase extraction model is proposed that captures the relatedness between words in terms of both mutual information and relevance feedback. Most of the existing works have stressed on bridging the semantic gap by using textual and visual features, either in combination or individually. The way these text and image features are combined determines the efficacy of any retrieval. For this purpose, Fisher-LDA is adapted to adjudge the appropriate weights for each modality. This provides us with an intelligent decision-making process favoring the feature set to be infused into the final query. This approach has shown to supersede the previously mentioned key phrase extraction algorithms for query expansion significantly (Datta et al 2017). However, the size of the search scope is unspecified. A few other image search engines have also been developed during the last few years. However, none of these techniques can dynamically combine text keyword and image feature at the time of retrieval.

In this chapter, a technique is presented for dynamic integration of keywords with FOS features for retrieval applications. In the proposed technique, a large number of HTML documents containing text and images available on the Internet are used. Using a crawler, the HTML documents are fetched. The content of the HTML documents is segregated into text, image and HTML tags. From the text, keywords are extracted and these keywords are considered as relevant keywords for representing high-level semantics of the images contained in the same HTML document.

IMAGE RETRIEVAL USING KEYWORDS AND FOS FEATURES

The semantics of an image can be described by a collection of one or more keywords. Let I be a set images and K be a set of keywords. Assignment of a keyword to an image may be treated as a labeling predicate written as follows:

$$l : K \times I \rightarrow \{True, False\} \tag{1}$$

Thus, a keyword $k \in K$ can be assigned to an image $i \in I$ if $l(k, i) = True$. Since a keyword can be assigned to multiple images and multiple keywords may be assigned to one image, given a subset of keywords $K' \subseteq K$, K' can be used to define a subset of images from I as follows.

$$C^I_{KD}(K') = \left\{ i \mid i \in I \ and \ \forall k \in K', l(k, i) = True \right\} \tag{2}$$

Various Boolean operations like OR, AND and NOT can be used for combining keywords. However, while performing retrieval, only Boolean ANDing of keywords in the query predicate alone is used. If we do not restrict the set of images by keyword, i.e. if $K' = \varphi$, $C^I_{KD}(\varphi) = I$ meaning that all the images in the database form one set. Thus, if images could be correctly labeled by a set of K keywords, retrieval based on a subset $K' \subseteq K$ of keywords would retrieve only relevant images resulting in 100% recall and precision. The main problem with such a keyword-based retrieval is that, it is not feasible to manually annotate each image with keywords. One of the difficulties lies in the fact that it is a subjective process. Different users may describe the same image in different ways. It is also language dependent. Further, it cannot be ensured that whoever is building the image database will also annotate it. If we consider the images available on the Web embedded in HTML documents, authors who have created any web page may not have correctly updated the image description while publishing the page. Even if it is done, it could be highly subjective as mentioned above. In contrast to keyword based retrieval, content based retrieval of images searches for images "similar" to a given query image with respect to suitable low-level features. Such features may be color, texture, shape or some suitable combination. The "similarity" between a query image and an image stored in a database based on a feature vector f is usually estimated with respect to a suitable distance function as described in Chapter 5. Hence, given a query image q, the set of images that are retrieved from the image database I using a feature vector f, a distance function d and a distance range Δd can be denoted by

$$Q\left(q,f,d,I,\Delta d\right) = \left\{ i \middle| i \in I \quad and \quad d\left(q,i\right) \le \Delta d \right\} \subseteq I \qquad (3)$$

Although each image in the set $Q\left(q,f,d,I,\Delta d\right)$ is within a distance of Δd from q, it cannot always be guaranteed that the images in $Q\left(q,f,d,I,\Delta d\right)$ are semantically close to q. Since precision of retrieval considers the set of images that are semantically relevant to the query image, content-based retrieval cannot guarantee high precision except in databases that contain a large number of images that are both semantically close as well as image feature wise close to a given query. We can refine content-based retrieval results by only selecting those images that match a set of keywords $K_1 \subseteq K$, if such keyword labeling is available. This leads to a composite content-based image retrieval scheme involving both keywords and image features. The images retrieved from an image database I, with a query involving a set of keywords $K_1 \subseteq K$ and an example image i may be denoted by

$$Q\left(K_1,q,f,d,I,\Delta d\right) = \left\{ i \in I \middle| d\left(q,i\right) \le \Delta d \quad and \quad \forall k \in K_1, l\left(k,i\right) = True \right\}$$
(4)

From Equations (2)-(4), it is defined as

$$Q\left(K_{1}, i, f, d, I, \Delta d\right) = C_{KD}^{I}\left(K_{1}\right) \cap Q\left(i, f, d, I, \Delta d\right) \tag{5}$$

Equation (5) represents the set of images that are labeled by each keyword from the set K_{1}, and are also close to the query image q in terms of the content of the feature f. If we perform nearest neighbor query, we can choose only those images that are labeled by the keywords of the set K_{1} and then rank them in increasing order of their distance from q with respect to feature f and distance function d. For a smaller subset $K_{1}^{'}$ of keywords such that $K_{1}^{'} \subseteq K_{1}$

$$Q\left(K_{1}, i, f, d_{f}, I, \Delta d_{f}\right) \subseteq Q\left(K_{1}^{'}, i, f, d_{f}, I, \Delta d_{f}\right) \tag{6}$$

As is evident from the above discussions, if a user can specify the keywords that describe his required set of images correctly and if the relevant database images are also labeled with the same set of keywords, we would achieve 100% recall and precision. However, due to the subjective nature of annotations, such high accuracy is not achieved in practice. On the other hand, since low-level features represent inherent content of images, there is little subjectivity in specifying them. The main drawback is the inability to capture complete high-level semantics in such low-level features. As a result, use of only low-level features is also not very accurate. Thus, while keywords help in reducing the search space, it would be interesting to find a minimal set of keywords that can be used along with low-level features to achieve a desired level of precision. Let $K_{1}^{'} \subset K_{1} \subseteq K$ be a set of keywords such that

$$C_{K}^{I}\left(K_{1}\right) = Q\left(K_{1}^{'}, i, f, d_{f}, I, \Delta d_{f}\right) \tag{7}$$

This implies that the set of images retrieved by using only the keywords K_{1} is the same as the set of images retrieved using a less number of keywords $K_{1}^{'}$ in conjunction with the image feature f. If such a subset $K_{1}^{'}$ can be found, we may say that the feature f represents the same semantics as that of the set of keywords $\left(K_{1} - K_{1}^{'}\right)$ with respect to the query image q and image database I. Experiments are performed on a keyword annotated image database to determine whether the same precision can be achieved using a smaller set of keywords and FOS feature. The retrieval performance of a keyword-only query is compared with a combined keyword and FOS feature query. For instance, consider a query with keywords 'cloudy sky', i.e. $K1=$ {cloudy, sky}. The retrieved images with this query are shown in Figure 1 (a). When the keyword 'cloudy' is replaced by an image of a cloudy sky (Figure 1 (e)) and the keyword sky is retained i.e. $K_1' =$ {sky} and q = an image of a cloudy sky, f=FOS feature, d=CBSM, the retrieval result from the same image database is shown in Figure 1(b). These two result sets although are not exactly the same, have close resemblance. Similar observation can be made from Figure 1(c) and (d). Here, retrieval based on the keywords 'sun in cloudy sky' is compared with that using the keyword 'sky' along with FOS feature of an image with sun and cloud (Figure 1(f)). Here also, the results show a lot of similarity. One may, therefore, conclude that with this image database, FOS feature associated with 'cloudy' images captures the semantics of 'cloudy' and FOS feature of sun and cloud images corresponds to the keyword 'sun cloud'.

PERFORMANCE EVALUATION

Initially, images from Corel database with 10,000 images having 100 categories are considered and the *FOS* feature of each image is treated as high dimensional data. The total number of vector is 10,000 *(FOSV)*, the dimension of each *FOSV* is 7 *(D)* and the total (P_{total}) is 70000. As mentioned earlier, most of the bin values of *FOSV* may have values zero or close to zero. This is due to the fact that the bin value of square is high for a square dominant image and other bin values may be zero or approximately zero. The points with zero values are discarded and only P_{Dist} points are used to represent P_{total} and thereby the feature is represented in a compact form. The first K-dominant dimension of query vector is identified, pattern is created and the clusters related to those patterns are retained for computing the *K-NN*. For comparison, the *FOS* of Corel database is extracted and they are maintained both in the normal form and indexed form. Here, the normal form is referred to as the feature vector stored in a sequence form and the indexed form is referred to as the proposed pattern based indexing structure. The performance is evaluated using three well-known metrics namely Precision, Recall and *F1* score. Precision is measured by retrieving the top-20 results for large number of queries and the average of the all the results is calculated. In Chapter 4, Figure 7, the average precision is shown for various nearest neighbors. The

Figure 1a. Retrieval result using keywords 'the cloudy sky'

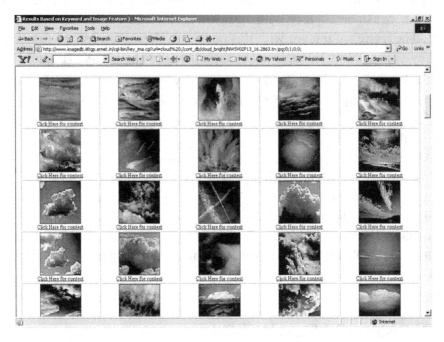

Figure 1b. Retrieval result using 'sky 'and a cloudy image

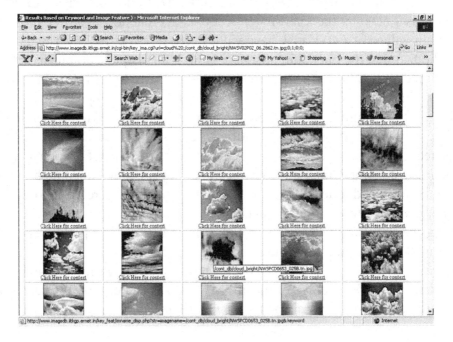

Figure 1c. Retrieval result using 'sun in cloudy sky' as keywords

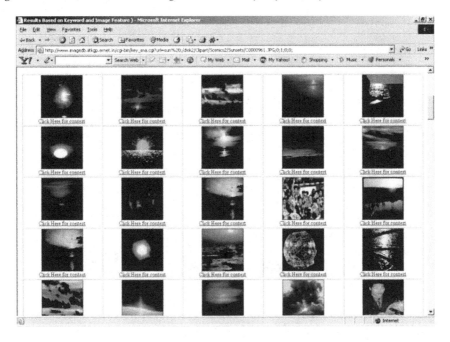

Figure 1d. Retrieval result using 'sky'and a blue color image

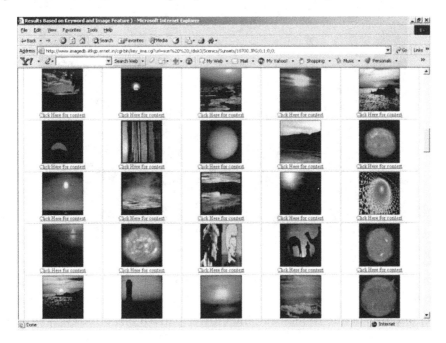

Figure 1e. Retrieval result cloudy image used

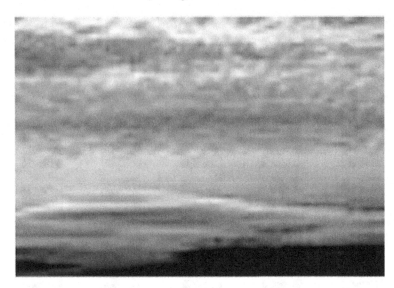

Figure 1f. Retrieval result of clouded sunny image

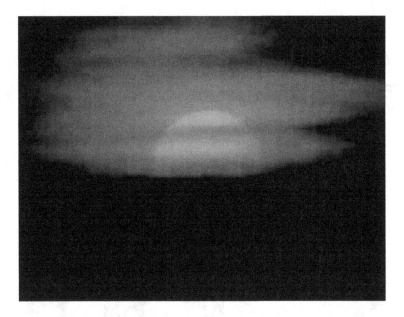

average precision of Indexed *FOS (IFOS)* and Linear *FOS (LFOS)* are similar up to top-15 *NN*. For 20 *NN*, the precision of *IFOS* is slightly better than the *LFOS* and this is due to fact that the cluster pattern has effectively grouped the images for improving the Precision of retrieval. In addition, the higher Precision of retrieval is achieved by comparing lesser number of features, which has reduced the retrieval time.

In Figure 2, the average Recall for various *NN* is depicted. The reason for performance enhancement is due to the capability of pattern based indexing scheme, where relevant images are grouped together effectively in a cluster, based on the shape categories. Based on all these experimental results, it is observed that the performance of the indexing approach is convincing as relevant images are indexed effectively using suitable pattern.

Performance Evaluation FOS Feature and Textual Information

The performance of the presented scheme is evaluated using uncontrolled database. Google (http://www.google.com) is a search engine with large number of indexed web pages and comparing the presented scheme with Google is more practical than searching in small-scale. The proposed approach has generated uncontrolled dataset using Google. This is done using a crawler that fetches and saves both the HTML pages and its related images. The reason for using web documents and images from WWW is that text information is extracted for indexing purpose (Sumathy & Vadivel,

Figure 2. Average recall of retrieval

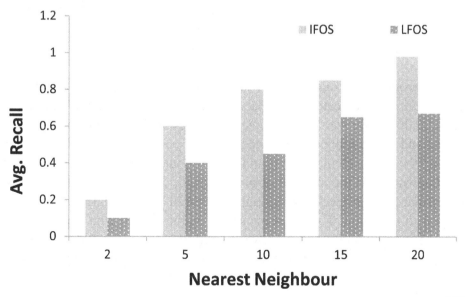

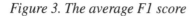

Figure 3. The average F1 score

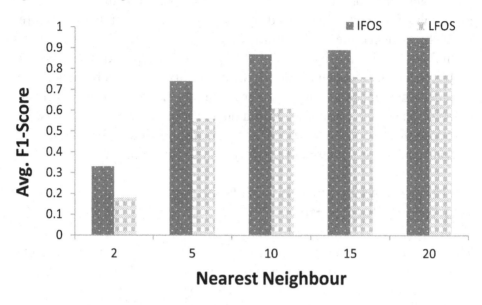

2016). In controlled image datasets, the text information may not be available for describing the image content. In contrast, the web document, in general uses text to describe the content of images. This is being considered as one of the primary reasons for using the crawled document. The terms related to various shapes are provided as query to the Google system and only the top-100 links are considered for evaluation process. This collection contains at least one qualified image in each web page. The URL links are given as input to the crawler for fetching those particular pages. The web pages associated with each query are saved in a separate repository, where all web pages in the same repository are semantically related and relevant to the same topic. The aim is to evaluate and investigate retrieval approaches using this heterogeneous collection of web pages that are browsed by users with various information categories. The total number of web pages in the dataset is 10,00,000 that cover various topics of interest and each page includes the mixed and overlapping of text/ images.

For the experiment, the ground truth about Google search engine is not known and in the absence of ground truth, the only way to present the performance objectively is through Perceived Precision *(PP)*, which is similar to Precision. The *PP* is measured by the person who is performing the queries. For a query, the person visually goes through the retrieval set by varying the *NN*. For each *NN*, the person finds out the relevant as well as irrelevant images and calculates PP. A group of post graduate students have performed the experiments and the Precision measured by the group is averaged and presented as result. Usually, online users are interested only in top-10 to top-100 web pages and *PP* is evaluated for these ranked web pages only. Since web pages contain text, images, etc., it is decided to evaluate the retrieval performance using text, *FOS* feature and combination of both.

The performance of text based retrieval using textual feature is shown in Figure 4. The *PP* for top 100 *NN* is presented from 10 *NN*. The average *PP* of the proposed approach is encouraging compared to Google. The performance deficiency of Google lies in the fact that it displays information from all commercial and social network pages within the top-100. For instance, while providing the keywords in Google say "Shape of a ball", the content from social networking pages like Facebook and Google+ are displayed on top-100. However, the proposed approach uses text information effectively, such that the relevant images alone are displayed on the top.

For image retrieval, Google Image search is used for comparison and its result is shown in Figure 5. The Google image search interface is used for image queries and the result is calculated. The same groups who have performed the text based query have performed this experiment also. It is

Figure 4. The average PP using textual feature as query

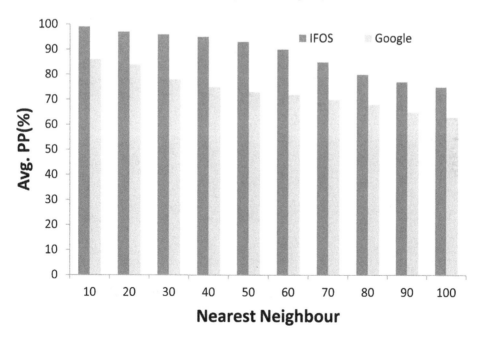

observed from the Figure 5, that the performance of the proposed approach is good compared to Google system. The reason for the improved performance is that the Google uses text information alone for describing the image content and the proposed approach uses the *FOS* for describing the image content.

Finally, both the text and *FOS* are combined together as query and the retrieval is shown in Figure 6. Here, only the performance of the proposed approach alone is presented and the reason is that there is no interface available to provide both the text and image feature in the Google system.

Based on all the above results, it is observed that the performance of the proposed approach is better compared to the popular search engine system. The reason is that the pattern based indexing for both textual and low-level features identifies the relevant images effectively.

Performance Evaluation Using Encoded FOS Feature

The effectiveness of the proposed encoded histogram is evaluated in an image retrieval system. For experiment, MIT benchmark dataset with 9356 images is

Figure 5. The average PP using FOS

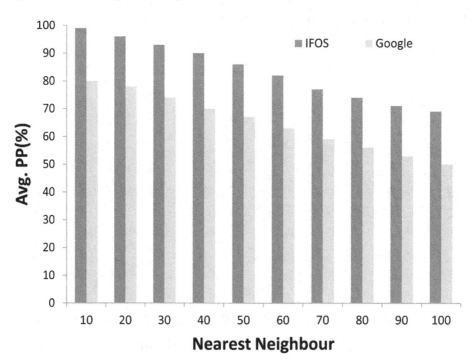

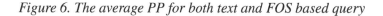

Figure 6. The average PP for both text and FOS based query

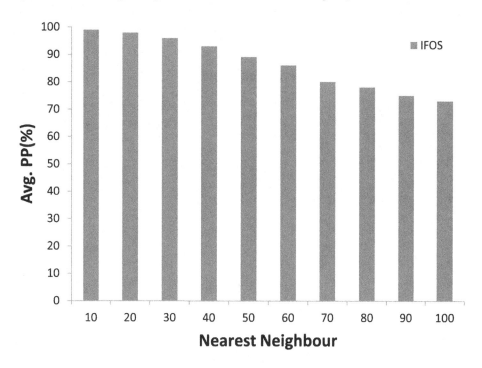

used in which 9144 object dominant images are categorized into 101 classes and 212 texture dominant images are categorized into 19 classes. Some query images from the various classes are selected randomly for computing Recall and Precision and considered top 50 retrieval images. The *CBSM* is used as the distance metric to measure the distance between query and distance images and for original normalized histogram. The Recall vs. Precision is depicted in Figure 7. (*a*) and it is observed that for lower values of Recall, the Precision is getting higher, which is reaching around 94%. The difference in Precision for various Recalls using encoded and original histogram is almost zero. Further to consolidate the performance of the proposed approach, the F-measure is calculated, which represents harmonic mean of Recall and precision. It can be noticed from the Figure 7. (*b*) that the difference in F-Measure of encoded and original histogram for various nearest neighbours is almost zero. This performance enhancement is due to the fact that the encoding procedure just assigns the code for minimizing the size of the histogram and the information is not lost. Thus, it is noticed that the proposed approach performs well and retrieves the same result set as original histogram but consumes less space thereby reducing the retrieval time.

Figure 7. Performance between original and encoded histograms (a) precision vs. recall (b) F-measure

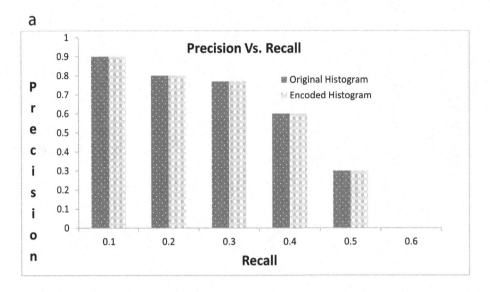

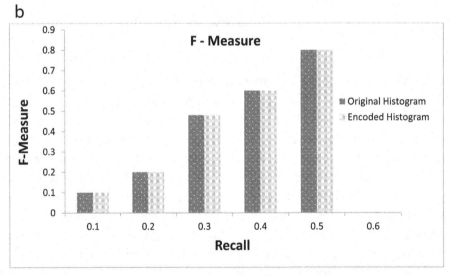

The sample retrieval results are shown in Figure 8 (*a*) and Figure 8 (*b*). The difference in the precision of retrieval for both of these histograms is negligible. This is because that while encoding the bin values, the important color information is very well retained and only unwanted bin value is truncated and considered for saving storage space.

Figure 8. Sample retrieval set of original and encoded histogram (a) retrieval sets using original histogram (b) retrieval set using encoded histogram

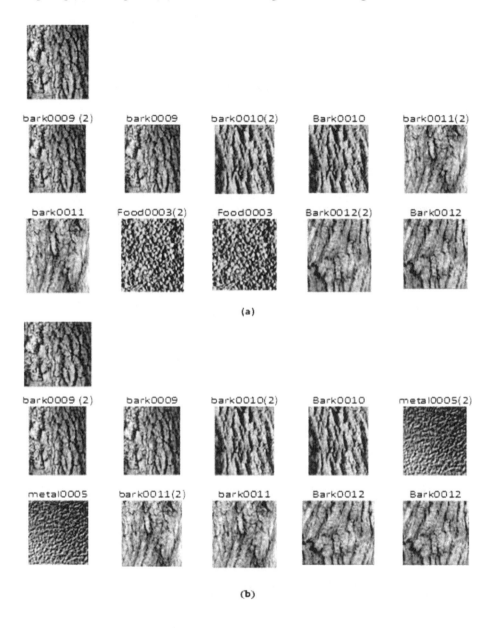

It is mentioned that the block indexed database gives better efficiency in retrieval time rather than flat database. Also, the entropy of *Q Code* and *C Code* are approximately same and as a result, *Q Code* alone is sufficient to represent the histogram. The performance comparison of *Q Code* and *C Code*

histograms is evaluated using block indexed and flat indexed databases. These evaluations are carried out on MIT benchmark dataset and it contains 9144 object dominant images (101 classes) and 212 texture dominant images (19

Figure 9. Retrieval performance of Q coded and C coded histograms using block indexed and flat database (a) precision (b)precision vs. recall

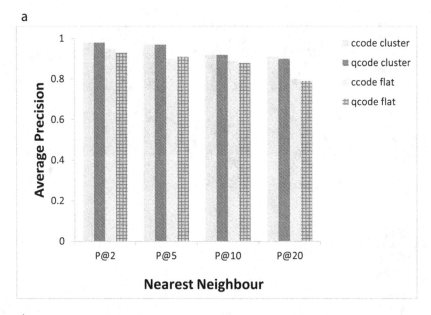

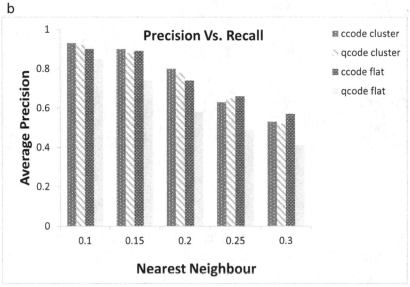

classes). Here, the dataset is segregated as two database structures such as block indexing structure and flat database structure. The ground truth varies for both of these structures in calculating Recall. The way by which the images are grouped gives the ground truth for the block indexed database. For the flat database structure, MIT dataset structure and its classes that are predefined earlier are considered as the ground truth. The *CBSM* is used as a distance metric between query and database image histograms. The object and texture dominant images are randomly selected as query images. During retrieval, *C Coded* histograms and *Q Code* histograms are considered individually for retrieving the images for a query. The performances of both *C Coded* histograms and *Q Code* histograms on block and flat indexed databases are evaluated.

CONCLUSION

In this Chapter, a method to combine both text and image feature is discussed. The FOS feature is discussed in Chapter 3 is combined with textual information extracted (as discussed in Chapter 1). A clustering mechanism is formulated based on image, text and both. A retrieval is presented as an example to demonstrate the functionality by which the reader can understand the use of combining both textual keywords and FOS. The Chapter has consolidated the performance of combined feature using Precision, Recall and F1-score. The performance is evaluated and compared with well-known Google retrieved system. The perceived precision is used as measure as there is no ground truth present with Google data. Along with, all the performance is also presented for encoded clustered FOS with text. Overall, the performance of the approach, to combine both the feature and text is encouraging compared to even Google.

REFERENCES

Bai, X., Shi, B., Zhang, C., & Cai, X. (2017). *Text*/non-*text image* classification in the wild with convolutional neural networks. *Pattern Recognition, 66,* 437–446.

Cui, , Lin, Nie, Yin, & Zhu. (2017). Textual-visual relevance learning for content-based image retrieval. *Journal of Visual Communication and Image Representation, 48,* 367–374.

Datta, D., Varma, S., Chowdary C, R., & Singh, S. K. (2017). Multimodal Retrieval using Mutual Information based Textual Query Reformulation Original research article. *Expert Systems with Applications, 68,* 81–92. doi:10.1016/j.eswa.2016.09.039

Deng, Y. (2001). An efficient colour representation for image retrieval. *IEEE Transactions on Image Processing, 10*(1), 140–147. doi:10.1109/83.892450 PMID:18249604

Gevers, T., & Stokman, H. M. G. (2004). Robust Histogram Construction from Color Invariants for Object Recognition. *IEEE Transactions on Pattern Analysis and Machine Intelligence, 26*(1), 113–118. doi:10.1109/TPAMI.2004.1261083 PMID:15382690

Shanmuga Vadivu, P., Sumathy P., & Vadivel, A. (2015). Shape of Objects in Images with Similarity Measure for Image Retrieval Applications. *International Journal of Computer Vision and Image Processing, 5*(2), 58-80.

Shanmuga Vadivu, P., Sumathy, P., & Vadivel, A. (2016). *FOSIR: Fuzzy-Object-Shape for Image Retrieval Applications. Journal Nuerocomputing, 171*(1), 719–735.

Sumathy, P., & Vadivel, A. (2016). Indexing and Encoding Fuzzy Shape Histogram with Common Bin Similarity Measure for CBIR Applications. *Proceedings of International Conference on Research in Engineering, Computers and Technology, (ICRECT'16),* 8-10.

Sumathy, P., & Vadivel, A. (2016). Textual and Shape based Features with Indexing Mechanisms for Image Retrieval: A Survey. CiiT International Journal of Image Processing, 8(8).

Vadivel, A., Shamik, S., & Majumdar, A. K. (2008). Robust Histogram Generation from the HSV Color Space based on Visual Perception. *International Journal on Signals and Imaging Systems Engineering, 1*(3/4), 245–254.

Vadivel, A., Sural, S., & Majumdar, A. K. (2007). An Integrated Color and Intensity Co-occurrence Matrix: *An Integrated Color and Intensity Co-Occurrence Matrix. Pattern Recognition Letters, 28*(8), 974–983. doi:10.1016/j.patrec.2007.01.004

Zhou, N., & Fan, J. (2015). Automatic image–text alignment for large-scale web image indexing and retrieval. *Pattern Recognition, 48*(1), 205–219. doi:10.1016/j.patcog.2014.07.001

Related Readings

To continue IGI Global's long-standing tradition of advancing innovation through emerging research, please find below a compiled list of recommended IGI Global book chapters and journal articles in the areas of image categorization, image processing, and coding imagery. These related readings will provide additional information and guidance to further enrich your knowledge and assist you with your own research.

Aggarwal, N., Rana, B., & Agrawal, R. (2014). Statistical Features-Based Diagnosis of Alzheimer's Disease using MRI. In M. Sarfraz (Ed.), *Computer Vision and Image Processing in Intelligent Systems and Multimedia Technologies* (pp. 38–53). Hershey, PA: IGI Global. doi:10.4018/978-1-4666-6030-4.ch003

Ahmed, N. (2017). Multi-View RGB-D Synchronized Video Acquisition and Temporally Coherent 3D Animation Reconstruction Using Multiple Kinects. In N. Dey, A. Ashour, & P. Patra (Eds.), *Feature Detectors and Motion Detection in Video Processing* (pp. 142–163). Hershey, PA: IGI Global. doi:10.4018/978-1-5225-1025-3.ch007

Ahmed, S. T. (2017). Managing Information, Communication and Technologies in Schools: Overload as Mismanagement and Miscommunication. In R. Marques & J. Batista (Eds.), *Information and Communication Overload in the Digital Age* (pp. 72–92). Hershey, PA: IGI Global. doi:10.4018/978-1-5225-2061-0.ch004

Al-Jarrah, M. A., & Al-Omari, F. A. (2016). Fast Video Shot Boundary Detection Technique based on Stochastic Model. *International Journal of Computer Vision and Image Processing*, 6(2), 1–17. doi:10.4018/IJCVIP.2016070101

Ali, A., Couceiro, M. S., Anter, A. M., & Hassanian, A. E. (2014). Evaluating an Evolutionary Particle Swarm Optimization for Fast Fuzzy C-Means Clustering on Liver CT Images. In M. Sarfraz (Ed.), *Computer Vision and Image Processing in Intelligent Systems and Multimedia Technologies* (pp. 1–21). Hershey, PA: IGI Global. doi:10.4018/978-1-4666-6030-4.ch001

AlShahrani, A. M., Al-Abadi, M. A., Al-Malki, A. S., Ashour, A. S., & Dey, N. (2017). Automated System for Crops Recognition and Classification. In N. Dey, A. Ashour, & S. Acharjee (Eds.), *Applied Video Processing in Surveillance and Monitoring Systems* (pp. 54–69). Hershey, PA: IGI Global. doi:10.4018/978-1-5225-1022-2.ch003

alZahir, S. (2014). A Fast New Rotation Insensitive WP-Based Method for Image Indexing and Retrieval. In M. Sarfraz (Ed.), *Computer Vision and Image Processing in Intelligent Systems and Multimedia Technologies* (pp. 234–246). Hershey, PA: IGI Global. doi:10.4018/978-1-4666-6030-4.ch013

Anter, A. M., Abu ElSoud, M., & Hassanien, A. E. (2014). Automatic Mammographic Parenchyma Classification According to BIRADS Dictionary. In M. Sarfraz (Ed.), *Computer Vision and Image Processing in Intelligent Systems and Multimedia Technologies* (pp. 22–37). Hershey, PA: IGI Global. doi:10.4018/978-1-4666-6030-4.ch002

Arsenio, A. M. (2014). Application of Computer Vision Techniques for Exploiting New Video Coding Mechanisms. In R. Srivastava, S. Singh, & K. Shukla (Eds.), *Research Developments in Biometrics and Video Processing Techniques* (pp. 156–182). Hershey, PA: IGI Global. doi:10.4018/978-1-4666-4868-5.ch008

Bag, S. (2017). A Nearest Opposite Contour Pixel Based Thinning Strategy for Character Images. In N. Dey, A. Ashour, & P. Patra (Eds.), *Feature Detectors and Motion Detection in Video Processing* (pp. 123–140). Hershey, PA: IGI Global. doi:10.4018/978-1-5225-1025-3.ch006

Baharadwaj, N., Wadhwa, S., Goel, P., Sethi, I., Arora, C. S., Goel, A., & Parthasarathy, H. et al. (2014). De-Noising, Clustering, Classification, and Representation of Microarray Data for Disease Diagnostics. In R. Srivastava, S. Singh, & K. Shukla (Eds.), *Research Developments in Computer Vision and Image Processing: Methodologies and Applications* (pp. 149–174). Hershey, PA: IGI Global. doi:10.4018/978-1-4666-4558-5.ch009

Barthakur, M., & Sarma, K. K. (2016). Incorporation of Depth in Two Dimensional Video Captures: Review of Current Trends and Techniques. In V. Santhi, D. Acharjya, & M. Ezhilarasan (Eds.), *Emerging Technologies in Intelligent Applications for Image and Video Processing* (pp. 88–109). Hershey, PA: IGI Global. doi:10.4018/978-1-4666-9685-3.ch004

Batista, J. C., & Marques, R. P. (2017). An Overview on Information and Communication Overload. In R. Marques & J. Batista (Eds.), *Information and Communication Overload in the Digital Age* (pp. 1–19). Hershey, PA: IGI Global. doi:10.4018/978-1-5225-2061-0.ch001

Bedi, P., Bansal, R., & Sehgal, P. (2014). Securing Biometrics Using Watermarking. In R. Srivastava, S. Singh, & K. Shukla (Eds.), *Research Developments in Biometrics and Video Processing Techniques* (pp. 65–89). Hershey, PA: IGI Global. doi:10.4018/978-1-4666-4868-5.ch004

Bera, T. K., & Nagaraju, J. (2014). Electrical Impedance Tomography (EIT): A Harmless Medical Imaging Modality. In R. Srivastava, S. Singh, & K. Shukla (Eds.), *Research Developments in Computer Vision and Image Processing: Methodologies and Applications* (pp. 235–273). Hershey, PA: IGI Global. doi:10.4018/978-1-4666-4558-5.ch013

Berke, B., Akarsu, G., & Obay, G. (2017). The Impact of Information and Communication Technologies on Economic Growth and Electricity Consumption: Evidence from Selected Balkan and Eastern European Countries. In R. Marques & J. Batista (Eds.), *Information and Communication Overload in the Digital Age* (pp. 176–200). Hershey, PA: IGI Global. doi:10.4018/978-1-5225-2061-0.ch008

Bhat, C. G., & Kopparapu, S. K. (2017). Creating Sound Glyph Database for Video Subtitling. In M. S., & V. V. (Eds.), Multi-Core Computer Vision and Image Processing for Intelligent Applications (pp. 136-154). Hershey, PA: IGI Global. doi:10.4018/978-1-5225-0889-2.ch005

Bhowmick, B. (2014). 3D Reconstruction Using Multiple View Stereo and a Brief Introduction to Kinect. In R. Srivastava, S. Singh, & K. Shukla (Eds.), *Research Developments in Computer Vision and Image Processing: Methodologies and Applications* (pp. 15–37). Hershey, PA: IGI Global. doi:10.4018/978-1-4666-4558-5.ch002

Borovikov, E., Vajda, S., Lingappa, G., & Bonifant, M. C. (2017). Parallel Computing in Face Image Retrieval: Practical Approach to the Real-World Image Search. In M. S., & V. V. (Eds.), Multi-Core Computer Vision and Image Processing for Intelligent Applications (pp. 155-189). Hershey, PA: IGI Global. doi:10.4018/978-1-5225-0889-2.ch006

C. J. P. (2017). An Overview of Text Information Extraction from Images. In N. Kumar, A. Sangaiah, M. Arun, & S. Anand (Eds.), Advanced Image Processing Techniques and Applications (pp. 32-60). Hershey, PA: IGI Global. doi:10.4018/978-1-5225-2053-5.ch002

Chakraborty, S., Patra, P. K., Maji, P., Ashour, A. S., & Dey, N. (2017). Image Registration Techniques and Frameworks: A Review. In N. Dey, A. Ashour, & S. Acharjee (Eds.), *Applied Video Processing in Surveillance and Monitoring Systems* (pp. 102–114). Hershey, PA: IGI Global. doi:10.4018/978-1-5225-1022-2.ch005

Chakraborty, S., Roy, M., & Hore, S. (2017). A Study on Different Edge Detection Techniques in Digital Image Processing. In N. Dey, A. Ashour, & P. Patra (Eds.), *Feature Detectors and Motion Detection in Video Processing* (pp. 100–122). Hershey, PA: IGI Global. doi:10.4018/978-1-5225-1025-3.ch005

Chandran, B., Aruna, P., & Loganathan, D. (2016). Lung Disease Classification by Novel Shape-Based Feature Extraction and New Hybrid Genetic Approach: Lung Disease Classification by Shape-Based Method. In V. Santhi, D. Acharjya, & M. Ezhilarasan (Eds.), *Emerging Technologies in Intelligent Applications for Image and Video Processing* (pp. 321–346). Hershey, PA: IGI Global. doi:10.4018/978-1-4666-9685-3.ch013

Chantrapornchai, C., & Preechasuk, J. (2017). Exploring Image and Video Steganography Based on DCT and Wavelet Transform. In N. Kumar, A. Sangaiah, M. Arun, & S. Anand (Eds.), *Advanced Image Processing Techniques and Applications* (pp. 61–89). Hershey, PA: IGI Global. doi:10.4018/978-1-5225-2053-5.ch003

Chaudhary, A., Raheja, J. L., Das, K., & Raheja, S. (2014). Fingers' Angle Calculation Using Level-Set Method. In M. Sarfraz (Ed.), *Computer Vision and Image Processing in Intelligent Systems and Multimedia Technologies* (pp. 191–202). Hershey, PA: IGI Global. doi:10.4018/978-1-4666-6030-4.ch010

Chiranjeevi, K., Jena, U., & Dash, S. (2017). Comparative Performance Analysis of Optimization Techniques on Vector Quantization for Image Compression. *International Journal of Computer Vision and Image Processing*, *7*(1), 19–43. doi:10.4018/IJCVIP.2017010102

D, E., & M, A. (2017). Fuzzy Approaches and Analysis in Image Processing. In N. Kumar, A. Sangaiah, M. Arun, & S. Anand (Eds.), *Advanced Image Processing Techniques and Applications* (pp. 1-31). Hershey, PA: IGI Global. doi:10.4018/978-1-5225-2053-5.ch001

D, J., & D, D. (2017). Background Subtraction and Object Tracking via Key Frame-Based Rotational Symmetry Dynamic Texture. In N. Kumar, A. Sangaiah, M. Arun, & S. Anand (Eds.), *Advanced Image Processing Techniques and Applications* (pp. 267-296). Hershey, PA: IGI Global. doi:10.4018/978-1-5225-2053-5.ch013

D'Avy, J., Hsu, W., Chen, C., Koschan, A. F., & Abidi, M. (2016). An Efficient Method for Optimizing Segmentation Parameters. In V. Santhi, D. Acharjya, & M. Ezhilarasan (Eds.), *Emerging Technologies in Intelligent Applications for Image and Video Processing* (pp. 29–47). Hershey, PA: IGI Global. doi:10.4018/978-1-4666-9685-3.ch002

Das, A. J., Saikia, N., & Sarma, K. K. (2016). Object Classification and Tracking in Real Time: An Overview. In V. Santhi, D. Acharjya, & M. Ezhilarasan (Eds.), *Emerging Technologies in Intelligent Applications for Image and Video Processing* (pp. 250–295). Hershey, PA: IGI Global. doi:10.4018/978-1-4666-9685-3.ch011

Dey, N., Ashour, A. S., & Hassanien, A. E. (2017). Feature Detectors and Descriptors Generations with Numerous Images and Video Applications: A Recap. In N. Dey, A. Ashour, & P. Patra (Eds.), *Feature Detectors and Motion Detection in Video Processing* (pp. 36–65). Hershey, PA: IGI Global. doi:10.4018/978-1-5225-1025-3.ch003

Dey, N., Nandi, B., Roy, A. B., Biswas, D., Das, A., & Chaudhuri, S. S. (2014). Analysis of Blood Smear and Detection of White Blood Cell Types Using Harris Corner. In R. Srivastava, S. Singh, & K. Shukla (Eds.), *Research Developments in Computer Vision and Image Processing: Methodologies and Applications* (pp. 357–370). Hershey, PA: IGI Global. doi:10.4018/978-1-4666-4558-5.ch017

Dhal, K. G., Sen, S., Sarkar, K., & Das, S. (2016). Entropy based Range Optimized Brightness Preserved Histogram-Equalization for Image Contrast Enhancement. *International Journal of Computer Vision and Image Processing*, 6(1), 59–72. doi:10.4018/IJCVIP.2016010105

Dhavale, S. V. (2017). *Advanced Image-Based Spam Detection and Filtering Techniques* (pp. 1–213). Hershey, PA: IGI Global. doi:10.4018/978-1-68318-013-5

Dhawale, C. A. (2017). Review and Applications of Multimodal Biometrics for Secured Systems. In N. Kumar, A. Sangaiah, M. Arun, & S. Anand (Eds.), *Advanced Image Processing Techniques and Applications* (pp. 251–266). Hershey, PA: IGI Global. doi:10.4018/978-1-5225-2053-5.ch012

Dhawale, C. A., & Jambhekar, N. D. (2017). Digital Image Steganography: Survey, Analysis, and Application. In N. Kumar, A. Sangaiah, M. Arun, & S. Anand (Eds.), *Advanced Image Processing Techniques and Applications* (pp. 324–346). Hershey, PA: IGI Global. doi:10.4018/978-1-5225-2053-5.ch015

Dubey, S. R., & Jalal, A. S. (2014). Automatic Fruit Disease Classification Using Images. In M. Sarfraz (Ed.), *Computer Vision and Image Processing in Intelligent Systems and Multimedia Technologies* (pp. 82–100). Hershey, PA: IGI Global. doi:10.4018/978-1-4666-6030-4.ch005

El Hariri, E., El-Bendary, N., Hassanien, A. E., & Badr, A. (2014). Automated Ripeness Assessment System of Tomatoes Using PCA and SVM Techniques. In M. Sarfraz (Ed.), *Computer Vision and Image Processing in Intelligent Systems and Multimedia Technologies* (pp. 101–130). Hershey, PA: IGI Global. doi:10.4018/978-1-4666-6030-4.ch006

Ellwart, T., & Antoni, C. H. (2017). Shared and Distributed Team Cognition and Information Overload: Evidence and Approaches for Team Adaptation. In R. Marques & J. Batista (Eds.), *Information and Communication Overload in the Digital Age* (pp. 223–245). Hershey, PA: IGI Global. doi:10.4018/978-1-5225-2061-0.ch010

Ezhilarasan, M., Nirmal, K. K., & Thambidurai, P. (2016). An Efficient Algorithm for Fast Block Motion Estimation in High Efficiency Video Coding. In V. Santhi, D. Acharjya, & M. Ezhilarasan (Eds.), *Emerging Technologies in Intelligent Applications for Image and Video Processing* (pp. 132–150). Hershey, PA: IGI Global. doi:10.4018/978-1-4666-9685-3.ch006

Gandhi, S., & Ratanpara, T. V. (2017). Object-Based Surveillance Video Synopsis Using Genetic Algorithm. In N. Dey, A. Ashour, & S. Acharjee (Eds.), *Applied Video Processing in Surveillance and Monitoring Systems* (pp. 193–219). Hershey, PA: IGI Global. doi:10.4018/978-1-5225-1022-2.ch009

Gandhi, U. D. (2017). A Novel Approach of Human Tracking Mechanism in Wireless Camera Networks. In N. Kumar, A. Sangaiah, M. Arun, & S. Anand (Eds.), *Advanced Image Processing Techniques and Applications* (pp. 297–323). Hershey, PA: IGI Global. doi:10.4018/978-1-5225-2053-5.ch014

Ganguin, S., Gemkow, J., & Haubold, R. (2017). Information Overload as a Challenge and Changing Point for Educational Media Literacies. In R. Marques & J. Batista (Eds.), *Information and Communication Overload in the Digital Age* (pp. 302–328). Hershey, PA: IGI Global. doi:10.4018/978-1-5225-2061-0.ch013

Geetha, M. K., Arunnehru, J., & Geetha, A. (2016). Early Recognition of Suspicious Activity for Crime Prevention. In V. Santhi, D. Acharjya, & M. Ezhilarasan (Eds.), *Emerging Technologies in Intelligent Applications for Image and Video Processing* (pp. 205–231). Hershey, PA: IGI Global. doi:10.4018/978-1-4666-9685-3.ch009

Geetha, P. (2014). Survey of Medical Image Compression Techniques and Comparative Analysis. In R. Srivastava, S. Singh, & K. Shukla (Eds.), *Research Developments in Computer Vision and Image Processing: Methodologies and Applications* (pp. 327–356). Hershey, PA: IGI Global. doi:10.4018/978-1-4666-4558-5.ch016

Giuliani, D. (2017). A Robust Skeletonization Method for Topological Complex Shapes. *International Journal of Computer Vision and Image Processing*, 7(1), 1–18. doi:10.4018/IJCVIP.2017010101

Goel, N., & Sehgal, P. (2016). Multi-Modal Fusion Schemes for Image Retrieval Systems to Bridge the Semantic Gap. In V. Santhi, D. Acharjya, & M. Ezhilarasan (Eds.), *Emerging Technologies in Intelligent Applications for Image and Video Processing* (pp. 151–184). Hershey, PA: IGI Global. doi:10.4018/978-1-4666-9685-3.ch007

Gómez, H. G., & Crespo, E. C. (2017). Photographers without Photographs: The Internet as Primary Resource. In R. Marques & J. Batista (Eds.), *Information and Communication Overload in the Digital Age* (pp. 44–70). Hershey, PA: IGI Global. doi:10.4018/978-1-5225-2061-0.ch003

Goswami, S., Dey, U., Roy, P., Ashour, A., & Dey, N. (2017). Medical Video Processing: Concept and Applications. In N. Dey, A. Ashour, & P. Patra (Eds.), *Feature Detectors and Motion Detection in Video Processing* (pp. 1–17). Hershey, PA: IGI Global. doi:10.4018/978-1-5225-1025-3.ch001

Hemalatha, S., & Anouncia, S. M. (2016). A Computational Model for Texture Analysis in Images with Fractional Differential Filter for Texture Detection. *International Journal of Ambient Computing and Intelligence, 7*(2), 93–113. doi:10.4018/IJACI.2016070105

Hore, S., Chatterjee, S., Chakraborty, S., & Shaw, R. K. (2017). Analysis of Different Feature Description Algorithm in object Recognition. In N. Dey, A. Ashour, & P. Patra (Eds.), *Feature Detectors and Motion Detection in Video Processing* (pp. 66–99). Hershey, PA: IGI Global. doi:10.4018/978-1-5225-1025-3.ch004

Ilangovan, S. S., Mahanty, B., & Sen, S. (2016). Biomedical Imaging Techniques. In V. Santhi, D. Acharjya, & M. Ezhilarasan (Eds.), *Emerging Technologies in Intelligent Applications for Image and Video Processing* (pp. 401–421). Hershey, PA: IGI Global. doi:10.4018/978-1-4666-9685-3.ch016

Irshad, M., Sarfraz, M., & Hussain, M. Z. (2014). Outline Capture of Planar Objects by Detecting Corner Features. In M. Sarfraz (Ed.), *Computer Vision and Image Processing in Intelligent Systems and Multimedia Technologies* (pp. 280–298). Hershey, PA: IGI Global. doi:10.4018/978-1-4666-6030-4.ch016

Jambulingam, V. K., & Santhi, V. (2017). Knowledge Discovery and Big Data Analytics: Issues, Challenges, and Opportunities. In A. Singh, N. Dey, A. Ashour, & V. Santhi (Eds.), *Web Semantics for Textual and Visual Information Retrieval* (pp. 144–164). Hershey, PA: IGI Global. doi:10.4018/978-1-5225-2483-0.ch007

Jameel, T., Lin, M., & Chao, L. (2016). Metamorphic Relations Based Test Oracles for Image Processing Applications. *International Journal of Software Innovation*, *4*(1), 16–30. doi:10.4018/IJSI.2016010102

Kandan, P., & Aruna, P. (2016). A New EYENET Model for Diagnosis of Age-Related Macular Degeneration: Diagnosis of Age-Related Macular Degeneration. In V. Santhi, D. Acharjya, & M. Ezhilarasan (Eds.), *Emerging Technologies in Intelligent Applications for Image and Video Processing* (pp. 422–440). Hershey, PA: IGI Global. doi:10.4018/978-1-4666-9685-3.ch017

Kang, L., Yu, C., Lin, C., & Yeh, C. (2016). Image and Video Restoration and Enhancement via Sparse Representation. In V. Santhi, D. Acharjya, & M. Ezhilarasan (Eds.), *Emerging Technologies in Intelligent Applications for Image and Video Processing* (pp. 1–28). Hershey, PA: IGI Global. doi:10.4018/978-1-4666-9685-3.ch001

Kansal, N., Solanki, V. K., & Kansal, V. (2017). Educational Data Mining and Indian Technical Education System: A Review. In N. Dey, A. Ashour, & P. Patra (Eds.), *Feature Detectors and Motion Detection in Video Processing* (pp. 18–34). Hershey, PA: IGI Global. doi:10.4018/978-1-5225-1025-3.ch002

Khaire, P. A., & Kotkondawar, R. R. (2017). Measures of Image and Video Segmentation. In N. Dey, A. Ashour, & S. Acharjee (Eds.), *Applied Video Processing in Surveillance and Monitoring Systems* (pp. 28–53). Hershey, PA: IGI Global. doi:10.4018/978-1-5225-1022-2.ch002

Khare, M., Srivastava, R. K., & Khare, A. (2014). Daubechies Complex Wavelet-Based Computer Vision Applications. In R. Srivastava, S. Singh, & K. Shukla (Eds.), *Research Developments in Biometrics and Video Processing Techniques* (pp. 138–155). Hershey, PA: IGI Global. doi:10.4018/978-1-4666-4868-5.ch007

Kim, H., Park, R., & Lee, J. (2014). Image Representation Using a Sparsely Sampled Codebook for Super-Resolution. In R. Srivastava, S. Singh, & K. Shukla (Eds.), *Research Developments in Computer Vision and Image Processing: Methodologies and Applications* (pp. 1–14). Hershey, PA: IGI Global. doi:10.4018/978-1-4666-4558-5.ch001

Kim, S. H., Park, R., Yang, S., & Kim, H. (2014). Feature-Based Affine Motion Estimation for Superresolution of a Region of Interest. In R. Srivastava, S. Singh, & K. Shukla (Eds.), *Research Developments in Biometrics and Video Processing Techniques* (pp. 118–137). Hershey, PA: IGI Global. doi:10.4018/978-1-4666-4868-5.ch006

Kneidinger-Müller, B. (2017). Perpetual Mobile Availability as a Reason for Communication Overload: Experiences and Coping Strategies of Smartphone Users. In R. Marques & J. Batista (Eds.), *Information and Communication Overload in the Digital Age* (pp. 93–119). Hershey, PA: IGI Global. doi:10.4018/978-1-5225-2061-0.ch005

Kolekar, M. K., Raja, G. L., & Sengupta, S. (2014). An Introduction to Wavelet-Based Image Processing and its Applications. In R. Srivastava, S. Singh, & K. Shukla (Eds.), *Research Developments in Computer Vision and Image Processing: Methodologies and Applications* (pp. 38–53). Hershey, PA: IGI Global. doi:10.4018/978-1-4666-4558-5.ch003

Krishnamoorthy, K., & Jeyabalu, M. (2017). A New Image Encryption Method Based on Improved Cipher Block Chaining with Optimization Technique. In N. Kumar, A. Sangaiah, M. Arun, & S. Anand (Eds.), *Advanced Image Processing Techniques and Applications* (pp. 133–149). Hershey, PA: IGI Global. doi:10.4018/978-1-5225-2053-5.ch006

Krishnamurthy, S., & Akila, V. (2017). Information Retrieval Models: Trends and Techniques. In A. Singh, N. Dey, A. Ashour, & V. Santhi (Eds.), *Web Semantics for Textual and Visual Information Retrieval* (pp. 17–42). Hershey, PA: IGI Global. doi:10.4018/978-1-5225-2483-0.ch002

Kumar, R., Pattnaik, P. K., & Pandey, P. (2017). Conversion of Higher into Lower Language Using Machine Translation. In A. Singh, N. Dey, A. Ashour, & V. Santhi (Eds.), *Web Semantics for Textual and Visual Information Retrieval* (pp. 92–107). Hershey, PA: IGI Global. doi:10.4018/978-1-5225-2483-0.ch005

Kumar, R., & Srivastava, R. (2014). Detection of Cancer from Microscopic Biopsy Images Using Image Processing Tools. In R. Srivastava, S. Singh, & K. Shukla (Eds.), *Research Developments in Computer Vision and Image Processing: Methodologies and Applications* (pp. 175–194). Hershey, PA: IGI Global. doi:10.4018/978-1-4666-4558-5.ch010

Kumar, R., Srivastava, R., & Srivastava, S. (2017). Microscopic Biopsy Image Segmentation Using Hybrid Color K-Means Approach. *International Journal of Computer Vision and Image Processing*, 7(1), 79–90. doi:10.4018/ IJCVIP.2017010105

Kumar, U. (2017). Significant Enhancement of Segmentation Efficiency of Retinal Images Using Texture-Based Gabor Filter Approach Followed by Optimization Algorithm. *International Journal of Computer Vision and Image Processing*, 7(1), 44–58. doi:10.4018/IJCVIP.2017010103

Kumar, V., Chhabra, J. K., & Kumar, D. (2014). Automatic MRI Brain Image Segmentation Using Gravitational Search-Based Clustering Technique. In R. Srivastava, S. Singh, & K. Shukla (Eds.), *Research Developments in Computer Vision and Image Processing: Methodologies and Applications* (pp. 313–326). Hershey, PA: IGI Global. doi:10.4018/978-1-4666-4558-5.ch015

Kushwaha, A. K., & Srivastava, R. (2014). Recognition of Humans and Their Activities for Video Surveillance. In R. Srivastava, S. Singh, & K. Shukla (Eds.), *Research Developments in Biometrics and Video Processing Techniques* (pp. 183–198). Hershey, PA: IGI Global. doi:10.4018/978-1-4666-4868-5.ch009

Ladjailia, A., Bouchrika, I., Harrati, N., & Mahfouf, Z. (2017). Encoding Human Motion for Automated Activity Recognition in Surveillance Applications. In N. Dey, A. Ashour, & S. Acharjee (Eds.), *Applied Video Processing in Surveillance and Monitoring Systems* (pp. 170–192). Hershey, PA: IGI Global. doi:10.4018/978-1-5225-1022-2.ch008

Lal, S. B., Sharma, A., Chaturvedi, K. K., Farooqi, M. S., Kumar, S., Mishra, D. C., & Jha, M. (2017). State-of-the-Art Information Retrieval Tools for Biological Resources. In A. Singh, N. Dey, A. Ashour, & V. Santhi (Eds.), *Web Semantics for Textual and Visual Information Retrieval* (pp. 203–226). Hershey, PA: IGI Global. doi:10.4018/978-1-5225-2483-0.ch010

Li, P., Lee, S., & Hsu, H. (2014). Use of Bi-Camera and Fusion of Pairwise Real Time Citrus Fruit Image for Classification Application. In M. Sarfraz (Ed.), *Computer Vision and Image Processing in Intelligent Systems and Multimedia Technologies* (pp. 54–81). Hershey, PA: IGI Global. doi:10.4018/978-1-4666-6030-4.ch004

López, M. B. (2017). Mobile Platform Challenges in Interactive Computer Vision. In M. S., & V. V. (Eds.), Multi-Core Computer Vision and Image Processing for Intelligent Applications (pp. 47-73). Hershey, PA: IGI Global. doi:10.4018/978-1-5225-0889-2.ch002

Lucas, M., & Moreira, A. A. (2017). Information and Communication Overload: Can DigComp Help? In R. Marques & J. Batista (Eds.), *Information and Communication Overload in the Digital Age* (pp. 157–175). Hershey, PA: IGI Global. doi:10.4018/978-1-5225-2061-0.ch007

M, V., & Thirugnanam, M. (2017). Shape Determination of Aspired Foreign Body on Pediatric Radiography Images Using Rule-Based Approach. In N. Kumar, A. Sangaiah, M. Arun, & S. Anand (Eds.), *Advanced Image Processing Techniques and Applications* (pp. 170-181). Hershey, PA: IGI Global. doi:10.4018/978-1-5225-2053-5.ch008

Mahmoud, T. M., Abd-El-Hafeez, T., & Omar, A. (2014). An Efficient System for Blocking Pornography Websites. In M. Sarfraz (Ed.), *Computer Vision and Image Processing in Intelligent Systems and Multimedia Technologies* (pp. 161–176). Hershey, PA: IGI Global. doi:10.4018/978-1-4666-6030-4.ch008

Maihami, V., & Yaghmaee, F. (2016). Color Features and Color Spaces Applications to the Automatic Image Annotation. In V. Santhi, D. Acharjya, & M. Ezhilarasan (Eds.), *Emerging Technologies in Intelligent Applications for Image and Video Processing* (pp. 378–400). Hershey, PA: IGI Global. doi:10.4018/978-1-4666-9685-3.ch015

Malhotra, M., & Singh, A. (2017). A Study on Models and Methods of Information Retrieval System. In A. Singh, N. Dey, A. Ashour, & V. Santhi (Eds.), *Web Semantics for Textual and Visual Information Retrieval* (pp. 43–68). Hershey, PA: IGI Global. doi:10.4018/978-1-5225-2483-0.ch003

Malik, K. R., & Ahmad, T. (2017). Technique for Transformation of Data From RDB to XML Then to RDF. In A. Singh, N. Dey, A. Ashour, & V. Santhi (Eds.), *Web Semantics for Textual and Visual Information Retrieval* (pp. 70–91). Hershey, PA: IGI Global. doi:10.4018/978-1-5225-2483-0.ch004

Manjunatha, K. C., Mohana, H. S., & Vijaya, P. A. (2014). Computer Vision-Based Non-Magnetic Object Detection on Moving Conveyors in Steel Industry through Differential Techniques and Performance Evaluation. In M. Sarfraz (Ed.), *Computer Vision and Image Processing in Intelligent Systems and Multimedia Technologies* (pp. 247–261). Hershey, PA: IGI Global. doi:10.4018/978-1-4666-6030-4.ch014

Maravilhas, S., & Martins, J. S. (2017). Information Management in Fab Labs: Avoiding Information and Communication Overload in Digital Manufacturing. In R. Marques & J. Batista (Eds.), *Information and Communication Overload in the Digital Age* (pp. 246–270). Hershey, PA: IGI Global. doi:10.4018/978-1-5225-2061-0.ch011

Marins, H. R., & Estrela, V. V. (2017). On the Use of Motion Vectors for 2D and 3D Error Concealment in H.264/AVC Video. In N. Dey, A. Ashour, & P. Patra (Eds.), *Feature Detectors and Motion Detection in Video Processing* (pp. 164–186). Hershey, PA: IGI Global. doi:10.4018/978-1-5225-1025-3.ch008

Mittal, N., Walia, E., & Singh, C. (2014). Magnitude and Phase of Discriminative Orthogonal Radial Moments for Face Recognition. In M. Sarfraz (Ed.), *Computer Vision and Image Processing in Intelligent Systems and Multimedia Technologies* (pp. 131–160). Hershey, PA: IGI Global. doi:10.4018/978-1-4666-6030-4.ch007

Moreno-Rabel, M. D., & Fernández-Muñoz, J. Á. (2017). Vision-Based Protective Devices. In N. Dey, A. Ashour, & P. Patra (Eds.), *Feature Detectors and Motion Detection in Video Processing* (pp. 187–214). Hershey, PA: IGI Global. doi:10.4018/978-1-5225-1025-3.ch009

Muraharirao, S. C., & Das, M. L. (2014). Securing Digital Image with Authentication Code. In M. Sarfraz (Ed.), *Computer Vision and Image Processing in Intelligent Systems and Multimedia Technologies* (pp. 203–215). Hershey, PA: IGI Global. doi:10.4018/978-1-4666-6030-4.ch011

Nagarajan, S. K., & Sangaiah, A. K. (2017). Vegetation Index: Ideas, Methods, Influences, and Trends. In N. Kumar, A. Sangaiah, M. Arun, & S. Anand (Eds.), *Advanced Image Processing Techniques and Applications* (pp. 347–386). Hershey, PA: IGI Global. doi:10.4018/978-1-5225-2053-5.ch016

Nair, S. A., & Aruna, P. (2016). Fingerprint Iris Palmprint Multimodal Biometric Watermarking System Using Genetic Algorithm-Based Bacterial Foraging Optimization Algorithm. In V. Santhi, D. Acharjya, & M. Ezhilarasan (Eds.), *Emerging Technologies in Intelligent Applications for Image and Video Processing* (pp. 347–376). Hershey, PA: IGI Global. doi:10.4018/978-1-4666-9685-3.ch014

Narang, S. K., Kumar, S., & Verma, V. (2017). Knowledge Discovery From Massive Data Streams. In A. Singh, N. Dey, A. Ashour, & V. Santhi (Eds.), *Web Semantics for Textual and Visual Information Retrieval* (pp. 109–143). Hershey, PA: IGI Global. doi:10.4018/978-1-5225-2483-0.ch006

Naskar, R., Chakraborty, R. S., Das, D. K., & Chakraborty, C. (2014). Digital Image Watermarking: Impact on Medical Imaging Applications in Telemedicine. In R. Srivastava, S. Singh, & K. Shukla (Eds.), *Research Developments in Computer Vision and Image Processing: Methodologies and Applications* (pp. 195–207). Hershey, PA: IGI Global. doi:10.4018/978-1-4666-4558-5.ch011

Nikkam, P. S., & Reddy, B. E. (2016). A Key Point Selection Shape Technique for Content Based Image Retrieval System. *International Journal of Computer Vision and Image Processing*, 6(2), 54–70. doi:10.4018/IJCVIP.2016070104

Ouadid, Y., Fakir, M., & Minaoui, B. (2016). Tifinagh Printed Character Recognition through Structural Feature Extraction. *International Journal of Computer Vision and Image Processing*, 6(2), 42–53. doi:10.4018/IJCVIP.2016070103

Pal, K., Ghosh, G., & Bhattacharya, M. (2014). Biomedical Watermarking: An Emerging and Secure Tool for Data Security and Better Tele-Diagnosis in Modern Health Care System. In R. Srivastava, S. Singh, & K. Shukla (Eds.), *Research Developments in Computer Vision and Image Processing: Methodologies and Applications* (pp. 208–234). Hershey, PA: IGI Global. doi:10.4018/978-1-4666-4558-5.ch012

Pal, R. (2014). Computational Models of Visual Attention: A Survey. In R. Srivastava, S. Singh, & K. Shukla (Eds.), *Research Developments in Computer Vision and Image Processing: Methodologies and Applications* (pp. 54–76). Hershey, PA: IGI Global. doi:10.4018/978-1-4666-4558-5.ch004

Pascoal, R. M., & Guerreiro, S. L. (2017). Information Overload in Augmented Reality: The Outdoor Sports Environments. In R. Marques & J. Batista (Eds.), *Information and Communication Overload in the Digital Age* (pp. 271–301). Hershey, PA: IGI Global. doi:10.4018/978-1-5225-2061-0.ch012

Patel, P., Jena, B., Sahoo, B., Patel, P., & Majhi, B. (2016). Study of Noise Removal Techniques for Digital Images. In V. Santhi, D. Acharjya, & M. Ezhilarasan (Eds.), *Emerging Technologies in Intelligent Applications for Image and Video Processing* (pp. 48–87). Hershey, PA: IGI Global. doi:10.4018/978-1-4666-9685-3.ch003

Poonguzhali, N., & Ezhilarasan, M. (2016). Iris Identification System: A New Perspective. In V. Santhi, D. Acharjya, & M. Ezhilarasan (Eds.), *Emerging Technologies in Intelligent Applications for Image and Video Processing* (pp. 232–249). Hershey, PA: IGI Global. doi:10.4018/978-1-4666-9685-3.ch010

Prabhakar, C. J., & Kumar, P. U. (2014). Image Enhancement and Restoration Methods for Underwater Images. In R. Srivastava, S. Singh, & K. Shukla (Eds.), *Research Developments in Computer Vision and Image Processing: Methodologies and Applications* (pp. 93–110). Hershey, PA: IGI Global. doi:10.4018/978-1-4666-4558-5.ch006

Prabhakar, C. J., & Mohana, S. H. (2014). Computer Vision Based Technique for Surface Defect Detection of Apples. In R. Srivastava, S. Singh, & K. Shukla (Eds.), *Research Developments in Computer Vision and Image Processing: Methodologies and Applications* (pp. 111–121). Hershey, PA: IGI Global. doi:10.4018/978-1-4666-4558-5.ch007

Prakash, S. (2014). A Brief Review on Recent Trends in Image Restoration. In R. Srivastava, S. Singh, & K. Shukla (Eds.), *Research Developments in Computer Vision and Image Processing: Methodologies and Applications* (pp. 77–92). Hershey, PA: IGI Global. doi:10.4018/978-1-4666-4558-5.ch005

Prasad, M. V., & Kavati, I. (2014). Biometric Authentication Based on Hand Vein Pattern. In R. Srivastava, S. Singh, & K. Shukla (Eds.), *Research Developments in Biometrics and Video Processing Techniques* (pp. 52–64). Hershey, PA: IGI Global. doi:10.4018/978-1-4666-4868-5.ch003

Puviarasan, N., & Bhavani, R. (2016). Indexing of Image Features Using Quadtree. In V. Santhi, D. Acharjya, & M. Ezhilarasan (Eds.), *Emerging Technologies in Intelligent Applications for Image and Video Processing* (pp. 185–203). Hershey, PA: IGI Global. doi:10.4018/978-1-4666-9685-3.ch008

Raj, A. N., & Mahesh, V. G. (2017). Zernike-Moments-Based Shape Descriptors for Pattern Recognition and Classification Applications. In N. Kumar, A. Sangaiah, M. Arun, & S. Anand (Eds.), *Advanced Image Processing Techniques and Applications* (pp. 90–120). Hershey, PA: IGI Global. doi:10.4018/978-1-5225-2053-5.ch004

Rajeswari, P. R., Raju, S. V., Ashour, A. S., & Dey, N. (2017). Insilico Approach for Epitope Prediction toward Novel Vaccine Delivery System Design. In N. Dey, A. Ashour, & P. Patra (Eds.), *Feature Detectors and Motion Detection in Video Processing* (pp. 256–266). Hershey, PA: IGI Global. doi:10.4018/978-1-5225-1025-3.ch012

Rajini, N. H., & Bhavani, R. (2016). Automatic Detection and Classification of Ischemic Stroke Using K-Means Clustering and Texture Features. In V. Santhi, D. Acharjya, & M. Ezhilarasan (Eds.), *Emerging Technologies in Intelligent Applications for Image and Video Processing* (pp. 441–461). Hershey, PA: IGI Global. doi:10.4018/978-1-4666-9685-3.ch018

Ramaiah, M., & Ray, B. K. (2017). A Technique to Approximate Digital Planar Curve with Polygon. In N. Kumar, A. Sangaiah, M. Arun, & S. Anand (Eds.), *Advanced Image Processing Techniques and Applications* (pp. 150–169). Hershey, PA: IGI Global. doi:10.4018/978-1-5225-2053-5.ch007

Rani, J., Kumar, R., Sarkar, A., & Talukdar, F. A. (2017). A Study on Various Image Processing Techniques and Hardware Implementation Using Xilinx System Generator. In N. Dey, A. Ashour, & P. Patra (Eds.), *Feature Detectors and Motion Detection in Video Processing* (pp. 215–230). Hershey, PA: IGI Global. doi:10.4018/978-1-5225-1025-3.ch010

Rico-Diaz, A. J., Rodriguez, A., Puertas, J., & Bermudez, M. (2017). Fish Monitoring, Sizing, and Detection Using Stereovision, Laser Technology, and Computer Vision. In M. S., & V. V. (Eds.), Multi-Core Computer Vision and Image Processing for Intelligent Applications (pp. 190-210). Hershey, PA: IGI Global. doi:10.4018/978-1-5225-0889-2.ch007

Rodriguez, A., Rico-Diaz, A. J., Rabuñal, J. R., & Gestal, M. (2017). Fish Tracking with Computer Vision Techniques: An Application to Vertical Slot Fishways. In M. S., & V. V. (Eds.), Multi-Core Computer Vision and Image Processing for Intelligent Applications (pp. 74-104). Hershey, PA: IGI Global. doi:10.4018/978-1-5225-0889-2.ch003

Roy, P., Patra, N., Mukherjee, A., Ashour, A. S., Dey, N., & Biswas, S. P. (2017). Intelligent Traffic Monitoring System through Auto and Manual Controlling using PC and Android Application. In N. Dey, A. Ashour, & S. Acharjee (Eds.), *Applied Video Processing in Surveillance and Monitoring Systems* (pp. 244–262). Hershey, PA: IGI Global. doi:10.4018/978-1-5225-1022-2.ch011

S., J. R., & Omman, B. (2017). A Technical Assessment on License Plate Detection System. In M. S., & V. V. (Eds.), *Multi-Core Computer Vision and Image Processing for Intelligent Applications* (pp. 234-258). Hershey, PA: IGI Global. doi:10.4018/978-1-5225-0889-2.ch009

S. P. S., T, R., & N, B. (2017). An Image De-Noising Method Based on Intensity Histogram Equalization Technique for Image Enhancement. In N. Kumar, A. Sangaiah, M. Arun, & S. Anand (Eds.), Advanced Image Processing Techniques and Applications (pp. 121-132). Hershey, PA: IGI Global. doi:10.4018/978-1-5225-2053-5.ch005

Saad, A. H., & Ali, A. A. (2017). An Overview of Steganography: "Hiding in Plain Sight. In N. Dey, A. Ashour, & S. Acharjee (Eds.), *Applied Video Processing in Surveillance and Monitoring Systems* (pp. 116–144). Hershey, PA: IGI Global. doi:10.4018/978-1-5225-1022-2.ch006

Saifuddin, M., Yeong, L. S., Phooi, S. K., & Li-Minn, A. (2014). Stereo Vision-Based Object Matching, Detection, and Tracking: A Review. In R. Srivastava, S. Singh, & K. Shukla (Eds.), *Research Developments in Biometrics and Video Processing Techniques* (pp. 91–117). Hershey, PA: IGI Global. doi:10.4018/978-1-4666-4868-5.ch005

Sarfraz, M. (2014). Detecting Corner Features of Planar Objects. In M. Sarfraz (Ed.), *Computer Vision and Image Processing in Intelligent Systems and Multimedia Technologies* (pp. 262–279). Hershey, PA: IGI Global. doi:10.4018/978-1-4666-6030-4.ch015

Sarkar, A., & Kumar, R. (2017). Study of Various Image Segmentation Methodologies: An Overview. In N. Dey, A. Ashour, & S. Acharjee (Eds.), *Applied Video Processing in Surveillance and Monitoring Systems* (pp. 1–27). Hershey, PA: IGI Global. doi:10.4018/978-1-5225-1022-2.ch001

Seal, A., Bhattacharjee, D., Nasipuri, M., & Basu, D. K. (2014). Thermal Human Face Recognition for Biometric Security System. In R. Srivastava, S. Singh, & K. Shukla (Eds.), *Research Developments in Biometrics and Video Processing Techniques* (pp. 1–24). Hershey, PA: IGI Global. doi:10.4018/978-1-4666-4868-5.ch001

Semary, N. A. (2014). An Efficient Color Image Encoding Scheme Based on Colorization. In M. Sarfraz (Ed.), *Computer Vision and Image Processing in Intelligent Systems and Multimedia Technologies* (pp. 216–233). Hershey, PA: IGI Global. doi:10.4018/978-1-4666-6030-4.ch012

Serrano-Puche, J. (2017). Developing Healthy Habits in Media Consumption: A Proposal for Dealing with Information Overload. In R. Marques & J. Batista (Eds.), *Information and Communication Overload in the Digital Age* (pp. 202–222). Hershey, PA: IGI Global. doi:10.4018/978-1-5225-2061-0.ch009

Sevugan, P., Purushotham, S., & Chandran, A. (2017). Expert System through GIS-Based Cloud. In N. Kumar, A. Sangaiah, M. Arun, & S. Anand (Eds.), *Advanced Image Processing Techniques and Applications* (pp. 387–398). Hershey, PA: IGI Global. doi:10.4018/978-1-5225-2053-5.ch017

Shet, S., Aswath, A. R., Hanumantharaju, M. C., & Gao, X. (2017). Design of Reconfigurable Architectures for Steganography System. In N. Dey, A. Ashour, & S. Acharjee (Eds.), *Applied Video Processing in Surveillance and Monitoring Systems* (pp. 145–168). Hershey, PA: IGI Global. doi:10.4018/978-1-5225-1022-2.ch007

Singh, A., Dey, N., & Ashour, A. S. (2017). Scope of Automation in Semantics-Driven Multimedia Information Retrieval From Web. In A. Singh, N. Dey, A. Ashour, & V. Santhi (Eds.), *Web Semantics for Textual and Visual Information Retrieval* (pp. 1–16). Hershey, PA: IGI Global. doi:10.4018/978-1-5225-2483-0.ch001

Singh, A., & Sharma, A. (2017). Web Semantics for Personalized Information Retrieval. In A. Singh, N. Dey, A. Ashour, & V. Santhi (Eds.), *Web Semantics for Textual and Visual Information Retrieval* (pp. 166–186). Hershey, PA: IGI Global. doi:10.4018/978-1-5225-2483-0.ch008

Singh, P. K., Das, S., Sarkar, R., & Nasipuri, M. (2016). Line Parameter based Word-Level Indic Script Identification System. *International Journal of Computer Vision and Image Processing*, 6(2), 18–41. doi:10.4018/IJCVIP.2016070102

Singh, P. K., Singh, R. S., & Rai, K. N. (2016). Wavelets with Application in Image Compression. In V. Santhi, D. Acharjya, & M. Ezhilarasan (Eds.), *Emerging Technologies in Intelligent Applications for Image and Video Processing* (pp. 111–131). Hershey, PA: IGI Global. doi:10.4018/978-1-4666-9685-3.ch005

Sk, K., Mukherjee, M., & Maitra, M. (2017). FPGA-Based Re-Configurable Architecture for Window-Based Image Processing. In M. S., & V. V. (Eds.), Multi-Core Computer Vision and Image Processing for Intelligent Applications (pp. 1-46). Hershey, PA: IGI Global. doi:10.4018/978-1-5225-0889-2.ch001

Srinivasa, K., Sowmya, B., Kumar, D. P., & Shetty, C. (2016). Efficient Image Denoising for Effective Digitization using Image Processing Techniques and Neural Networks. *International Journal of Applied Evolutionary Computation*, 7(4), 77–93. doi:10.4018/IJAEC.2016100105

Srivastava, S., Sharma, N., & Singh, S. (2014). Image Analysis and Understanding Techniques for Breast Cancer Detection from Digital Mammograms. In R. Srivastava, S. Singh, & K. Shukla (Eds.), *Research Developments in Computer Vision and Image Processing: Methodologies and Applications* (pp. 123–148). Hershey, PA: IGI Global. doi:10.4018/978-1-4666-4558-5.ch008

Sudha, L. R., & Bhavani, R. (2016). Gait Based Biometric Authentication System with Reduced Search Space. In V. Santhi, D. Acharjya, & M. Ezhilarasan (Eds.), *Emerging Technologies in Intelligent Applications for Image and Video Processing* (pp. 296–320). Hershey, PA: IGI Global. doi:10.4018/978-1-4666-9685-3.ch012

Sultana, M., Paul, P. P., & Gavrilova, M. L. (2014). Online User Interaction Traits in Web-Based Social Biometrics. In M. Sarfraz (Ed.), *Computer Vision and Image Processing in Intelligent Systems and Multimedia Technologies* (pp. 177–190). Hershey, PA: IGI Global. doi:10.4018/978-1-4666-6030-4.ch009

T, P., & Nair, J. (2017). Diophantine Equations for Enhanced Security in Watermarking Scheme for Image Authentication. In N. Kumar, A. Sangaiah, M. Arun, & S. Anand (Eds.), *Advanced Image Processing Techniques and Applications* (pp. 205-229). Hershey, PA: IGI Global. doi:10.4018/978-1-5225-2053-5.ch010

Terra, A. L. (2017). Email Overload: Framing the Concept and Solving the Problem – A Literature Review. In R. Marques & J. Batista (Eds.), *Information and Communication Overload in the Digital Age* (pp. 20–43). Hershey, PA: IGI Global. doi:10.4018/978-1-5225-2061-0.ch002

Thontadari, C., & Prabhakar, C. J. (2016). Scale Space Co-Occurrence HOG Features for Word Spotting in Handwritten Document Images. *International Journal of Computer Vision and Image Processing*, 6(2), 71–86. doi:10.4018/IJCVIP.2016070105

Tiwari, S., & Singh, S. K. (2014). Multimodal Biometrics Recognition for Newborns. In R. Srivastava, S. Singh, & K. Shukla (Eds.), *Research Developments in Biometrics and Video Processing Techniques* (pp. 25–51). Hershey, PA: IGI Global. doi:10.4018/978-1-4666-4868-5.ch002

Tiwari, S., & Srivastava, R. (2014). Research and Developments in Medical Image Reconstruction Methods and its Applications. In R. Srivastava, S. Singh, & K. Shukla (Eds.), *Research Developments in Computer Vision and Image Processing: Methodologies and Applications* (pp. 274–312). Hershey, PA: IGI Global. doi:10.4018/978-1-4666-4558-5.ch014

Torsi, S. (2017). The Fishtank Paradigm of Experience: Merging Time, Space, Activities, Emotions, and People. In R. Marques & J. Batista (Eds.), *Information and Communication Overload in the Digital Age* (pp. 120–156). Hershey, PA: IGI Global. doi:10.4018/978-1-5225-2061-0.ch006

Upadhyay, S., Tiwari, S., & Parashar, S. (2014). Video Authentication: An Intelligent Approach. In R. Srivastava, S. Singh, & K. Shukla (Eds.), *Research Developments in Biometrics and Video Processing Techniques* (pp. 199–231). Hershey, PA: IGI Global. doi:10.4018/978-1-4666-4868-5.ch010

Urrea, C., & Araya, H. (2017). New Redundant Manipulator Robot with Six Degrees of Freedom Controlled with Visual Feedback. In N. Dey, A. Ashour, & P. Patra (Eds.), *Feature Detectors and Motion Detection in Video Processing* (pp. 231–255). Hershey, PA: IGI Global. doi:10.4018/978-1-5225-1025-3.ch011

Urrea, C., & Solar, G. (2017). Evaluation of Image Detection and Description Algorithms for Application in Monocular SLAM. In N. Kumar, A. Sangaiah, M. Arun, & S. Anand (Eds.), *Advanced Image Processing Techniques and Applications* (pp. 182–204). Hershey, PA: IGI Global. doi:10.4018/978-1-5225-2053-5.ch009

Urrea, C., & Uren, V. (2017). Technical Evaluation, Development, and Implementation of a Remote Monitoring System for a Golf Cart. In N. Dey, A. Ashour, & S. Acharjee (Eds.), *Applied Video Processing in Surveillance and Monitoring Systems* (pp. 220–243). Hershey, PA: IGI Global. doi:10.4018/978-1-5225-1022-2.ch010

Urrea, C., & Yau, A. (2017). Design, Construction, and Programming of a Mobile Robot Controlled by Artificial Vision. In N. Kumar, A. Sangaiah, M. Arun, & S. Anand (Eds.), *Advanced Image Processing Techniques and Applications* (pp. 230–250). Hershey, PA: IGI Global. doi:10.4018/978-1-5225-2053-5.ch011

Ursyn, A. (2014). *Perceptions of Knowledge Visualization: Explaining Concepts through Meaningful Images* (pp. 1–418). Hershey, PA: IGI Global. doi:10.4018/978-1-4666-4703-9

Vadhanam, B. R. S., M., Sugumaran, V., V., V., & Ramalingam, V. V. (2017). Computer Vision Based Classification on Commercial Videos. In M. S., & V. V. (Eds.), Multi-Core Computer Vision and Image Processing for Intelligent Applications (pp. 105-135). Hershey, PA: IGI Global. doi:10.4018/978-1-5225-0889-2.ch004

Vasavi, S., Jyothi, T. N., & Rao, V. S. (2017). Moving Object Classification in a Video Sequence. In N. Dey, A. Ashour, & S. Acharjee (Eds.), *Applied Video Processing in Surveillance and Monitoring Systems* (pp. 70–101). Hershey, PA: IGI Global. doi:10.4018/978-1-5225-1022-2.ch004

Veerapathiran, N., & Anand, S. (2017). Reducing False Alarms in Vision-Based Fire Detection. In N. Dey, A. Ashour, & S. Acharjee (Eds.), *Applied Video Processing in Surveillance and Monitoring Systems* (pp. 263–290). Hershey, PA: IGI Global. doi:10.4018/978-1-5225-1022-2.ch012

Vijayakumar, S., Dasari, N., Bhushan, B., & Reddy, R. (2017). Semantic Web-Based Framework for Scientific Workflows in E-Science. In A. Singh, N. Dey, A. Ashour, & V. Santhi (Eds.), *Web Semantics for Textual and Visual Information Retrieval* (pp. 187–202). Hershey, PA: IGI Global. doi:10.4018/978-1-5225-2483-0.ch009

Vijayakumar, S., & Thakare, V. R. J, A., Bhushan, S. B., & Santhi, V. (2017). Role of Social Networking Sites in Enhancing Teaching Environment. In A. Singh, N. Dey, A. Ashour, & V. Santhi (Eds.), Web Semantics for Textual and Visual Information Retrieval (pp. 227-243). Hershey, PA: IGI Global. doi:10.4018/978-1-5225-2483-0.ch011

About the Authors

P. Sumathy is Assistant Professor at Department of Computer Science, Bharathidasan University, Tiruchirappalli. She has completed M.Sc in Computer Science, M.Phil in Computer Science and Ph.D in the area of Image Retrieval. She has around 10 years of teaching experience and 7 years of research experience. She specializes in Content based Image Retrieval, Multimedia Information Retrieval and Data Mining. She has published several research papers in national and international journals of repute.

P. Shanmugavadivu is currently the Professor and Head, Department of Computer Science & Applications, at Gandhigram Rural Institute (Deemed University), and is involved in Teaching, Research, and Extension. She is the Local Coordinator for the University, for the Global Initiative of Academic Networks of MHRD, India. Dr. Pichai has 25+ years of Academic experience, and has guided/guiding Research Scholars, and funded-research projects of UGC, DST and ICMR. She has conducted a national conference, trainings, and workshops, and has delivered 80+ lectures as Keynote Speaker, Chief Guest, and Guest Lecturer. She has edited three volumes of research publications and two national journals, and authored about 100 research publications. Recipient of Indo-US 21st Century Knowledge Initiative Award 2015. She had been on an international academic assignment in Malaysia and USA. Dr. Pichai holds a Master's degree in Computer Applications from Regional Engineering College, Trichy, Ph.D. in Digital Image Restoration, and MBA.

A. Vadivel is currently working as Associate Professor at Department of Computer Science and Engineering, SRM University, Amaravati, AP, India. He has completed his M.Tech and Ph. D in Indian Institute of Technology, Kharagpur. He has around 11 years of Teaching Experience and 17 years of research experience. He has received Fast Track – Young Scientist Award by DST in 2007 and Indo-Us Research Fellow Award by Indo-US Science and Technology Forum in 2008. Also he received Obama-Singh Knowledge Initiative Award in 2013. He is the reviewer of many reputed journals like Elsevier, PAAA Springer, Imaging Science Journal, IEEE transaction on Cloud Computing, IET Computer Vision, Electronic Imaging, SPIE and IEEE Systems. Dr. A. Vadivel previously worked as Associate Professor, National Institute of Technology, Tiruchirappalli and Assistant Professor, Bharathidasan University, Trichy. He completed many funded research projects under DST, MHRD and United States – India Education Foundation. He has published around 94 research papers in reputed journals.

Index

A

algorithm 3, 9, 12, 40, 42, 49, 88-90, 118-120, 123, 125, 138

applications 1, 3, 5-6, 9-10, 12-13, 31, 34, 39-41, 47, 57, 62-64, 83, 87-89, 137-138, 140

B

Benchmark 47-48, 50, 53, 55, 57, 76, 80-81, 108-109, 150, 154

boundary 45, 57, 62-64, 66, 75, 83

C

categories 10, 21, 28, 41, 43, 47, 51-53, 56, 77, 79, 81, 88, 104-105, 107, 143, 147-148

CBIR 1-2, 4-5, 11, 39-41, 43, 57, 63, 83, 97, 139

code 30, 90, 99, 101-104, 109-110, 113-114, 130, 132, 151, 153, 155

Coefficient 51-52, 76, 78, 126

D

data 3, 5, 7, 9-11, 27, 39, 51-53, 57, 63, 78-79, 83-84, 88-89, 100, 104, 119-120, 127, 134, 143, 155

database 2, 4-5, 8, 10, 14-15, 28, 39-41, 43, 46-47, 50, 52-53, 55-57, 75-76, 78-81, 83, 87-89, 92, 94-95, 97, 100, 104-105, 109, 111-112, 114-115, 118, 123-130, 134, 140-143, 147, 153-155

E

encoding 87, 90-91, 97-98, 100, 102, 109, 113-115, 132, 151-152

Equation 14-18, 22, 25-26, 32, 45-46, 66-67, 69-71, 91-92, 99-100, 102-103, 113, 123, 129-131, 142

example 2, 4, 9, 16-17, 46, 91, 118, 134, 137-138, 141, 155

F

feature 3-5, 7, 9-11, 16, 39-44, 46-47, 49-50, 56-57, 62-64, 75, 82-84, 87-97, 99-100, 104-105, 107-109, 113-115, 118, 123, 125-127, 134, 137, 139-143, 147, 149-150, 155

FOSIR 64, 75-78, 80-81, 83, 127

function 17, 57, 62, 64, 66-67, 69-71, 82, 84, 120, 127, 141-142

Fuzzy-Object-Shape 63-64, 82-83, 89, 91

G

geometry 40, 52, 63, 79

H

high-level 1, 10, 15-16, 33, 140, 142

histogram 5, 8, 40-41, 90-91, 97-104, 108-109, 113, 129-131, 137, 150-151, 153

HTML 1, 7-8, 10-13, 15-19, 21, 23-26, 29, 31-34, 53, 80, 94, 105, 140-141, 147

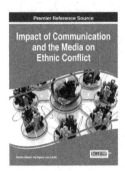

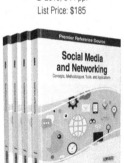
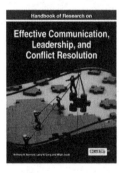

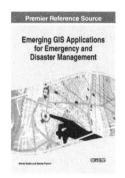
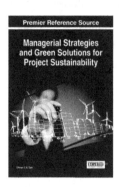

Printed in the United States
By Bookmasters